A PARTY REBORN

Governor Harold Hughes, 1964
UNIVERSITY OF IOWA ARCHIVES

A PARTY REBORN
THE DEMOCRATS OF IOWA
1950-1974

By
JAMES C. LAREW

IOWA STATE HISTORICAL DEPARTMENT
DIVISION OF THE STATE HISTORICAL SOCIETY
1980

Copyright © 1980 by the Iowa State Historical
Department/Division of the State Historical Society,
402 Iowa Avenue, Iowa City, Iowa 52240. Composed,
printed, and bound in the United States of America.
All rights reserved. No portion of this book may be
reproduced without permission of the publisher except
short citations for review purposes.

Library of Congress Card Catalog No: 80-51855
ISBN 0-89033-002-6

Editing, proofreading, and design: Charles Phillips
Production: William Silag and the Editorial Staff of the
   Iowa State Historical Department/Division of the
   State Historical Society
Line drawings: Dennett-Muessig Associates
Cover illustrations: Backroom Graphics, Inc.

ACKNOWLEDGEMENTS

I am grateful for the kindnesses extended to me by many persons and institutions who helped in the preparation of this manuscript, including:

— Harvard University and the John F. Kennedy Institute of Politics, which supported my earliest research efforts, and, in particular, my history tutor and good friend, Mr. Alan Brinkley;

— The people of Iowa, who, as thoughtful guardians of their history, continue to back the important work of the State Historical Society;

— The Director and staff members of the State Historical Society who have assisted me with the countless production details necessary to publish this book;

— The workers and leaders of Iowa's Democratic Party, who, through their efforts, have made this story one worth telling;

— And, the friends and members of my family who have encouraged my studies and activities in Iowa politics, especially my wife, Mary.

— JIM LAREW
March 25, 1980

*To my grandparents,
Telford and Irene Larew
and
Elmer K. and Grace Bekman*

A PARTY REBORN

CONTENTS

I Introduction: Iowa Politics and the Progressive Instinct   1

II Urbanization and the Silent Democrats   11

III Stirrings in Polk County: Democrats of the 1950s   37

IV The Democrats Reborn: The Rise of Harold Hughes   73

V The Organized Democrats: John Culver, Dick Clark, and the New Party Machinery   127

Notes   177

Bibliography   199

Index   207

"Iowa will go Democratic when Hell goes Methodist."
—Jonathan P. Dolliver, U.S. Senator from Iowa, 1885

The Iowa General Assembly
STATE HISTORICAL SOCIETY OF IOWA

I
INTRODUCTION: IOWA POLITICS AND THE PROGRESSIVE INSTINCT

FROM 1950 TO 1974 THE STATE OF IOWA witnessed a startling and dramatic change in its politics. In that brief time span, Iowans transformed their century-long tradition of one-party, Republican dominance into a new era of intense two-party competition. Democrats had controlled the state a few years before the Civil War, and they had enjoyed brief successes during moments of economic hard times in the late 19th Century and during the Great Depression. But their resurgence in the post-World War II era represented an entirely different phenomenon: a rebirth of resilient Democratic spirit anchored in an organization of unprecedented strength and sophistication.

Many complex and interrelated causes spurred the rejuvenation of Democratic politics in Iowa. No doubt the increased power of the national Democratic Party in the Depression and postwar years boosted the Iowa party. But, in addition to those larger trends, several crucial factors — characteristics special to Iowa's own history, issues, and personalities — aided efforts of Iowa Democrats to capture and then to guide political currents in the state.

Four important developments contributed to Democratic gains starting in the 1950s. First, progressive instincts had existed throughout Iowa's history. Finding their expression in third party movements in the 19th Century, later fighting for release against "standpatters" within the

A PARTY REBORN
− 2 −

Republican Party itself into the early 20th Century, by the 1950s those instincts were nearly smothered by powerful conservative interests within the Republican Party. In particular, Iowa's growing cities lacked proportional elective representation in the state's politics, and many persons from urban areas, often in frustration, now looked to the Democratic Party to provide a progressive voice. Second, Democrats developed organizational strategies and techniques in urban politics which led to the establishment of their first solid political base in Iowa's most populous city, Des Moines. Third, the Democrats expanded their appeal to other parts of the state, especially in the larger cities. The charismatic leader, Harold E. Hughes, became a familiar and popular figure thundering across Iowa's political landscape in numerous campaigns. Hughes's three consecutive terms as governor and his election to the United States Senate provided the party with strong and effective leadership grounded in progressive causes ignored or abused by other politicians for several decades. And finally, John C. Culver and his assistant Dick Clark of the Second Congressional District combined the organizational lessons learned by the Polk County Democrats with their own forceful approaches to politics. Under Culver and Clark, the methods of organizational politics were expanded and refined. New technologies employed by them brought Iowa Democrats into the computer age. Using these methods in their own statewide campaigns, both Clark and Culver were elected to the United States Senate, and Iowa Democrats enjoyed their greatest political successes since before the Civil War.

Democrats had dominated politics in Iowa when the territory joined the Union as a free state in 1846. But subsequent waves of Middle Atlantic and New England Protestant immigrants and Iowa's own intensive involvement in

INTRODUCTION

the Civil War changed the political orientation of the state. In the war, only Indiana's soldiers suffered a higher mortality rate than Iowa's.[1] For generations thereafter vivid memories of the conflict placed a shroud of disgrace upon the party of "Copperhead" Democrats who had opposed the Union Army war efforts. As a result, for nearly half a century political dissidents expressed their opposition to Republican Party policies not through the Democratic Party but either through third party movements or through divisions within the Grand Old Party itself.

From the Civil War until the New Deal era, then, surges of third party agrarian radicalism (which included Grangers, Greenbackers, and Populists) and fights between Republican "progressives" and "standpatters" provided the essential dimensions to Iowa's politics, a tradition bereft of a strong Democratic Party. No two of these movements — nor even any single movement over several years' time — appealed to the same constituency. Yet two characteristics linked every progressive period of protest. First, each movement expressed deeply-felt responses to an urbanizing and industrializing America whose political system often seemed ill-attuned to the new needs of the state's citizens. Second, in each movement Iowans fought to limit the growing powers of economic interest groups. To do so, they joined moral appeals with concrete plans to democratize further the economy, politics and government.[2] In the Granger, Anti-Monopoly, and Protective Association movements of the 1870s Iowans established an important political precedent for their state: the right of citizens through governmental and legal action to curb the excesses of private interests. After powerful railroad magnates and business concerns (barbed wire fence manufacturers, in particular) had refused to moderate the costs charged to farmers amidst severe agricultural market price

A PARTY REBORN
— 4 —

recessions, members of Iowa's enormous state Grange (Patrons of Husbandry) united to form the Anti-Monopoly Party. By 1873, over 50,000 Grangers located in nearly every county of the state pushed for anti-monopoly legislation. In the elections that year, the Grangers captured eight of 22 state Senate positions, and a majority of the Iowa House. In 1874, Grangers in the Iowa General Assembly established maximum rate schedules for railroad grain shipments. Charles Eliot Perkins, powerful president of the Burlington Railroad, objected to the Granger laws' provisions and employed his considerable influence in the General Assembly to have the statutes altered in 1878. The Grangers, however, while losing their laws, retained the principle of railroad regulation by establishing a commission that same year to investigate alleged railroad abuses. By the 1880s, after experimenting with manufacturing industries owned by cooperatives, the Grange fell into bankruptcy and the Anti-Monopoly Party collapsed in disarray.[3] But the momentum they had established carried progressive impulses into the next decade. In 1881, farmers formed a "Protective Association" to test in court the legality of monopolistic practices in the barbed wire industry. Five years later, now with the blessings of the courts, the power of the monopoly was broken.

In the meantime, as the Granger movement dissipated after its initial battles with the railroads, farmers still suffered from the low grain prices of glutted markets, and some Iowans continued to seek non-Republican political alternatives. Many sought government relief from their debts through national inflationary monetary policies. In 1878, no state in the nation equalled Iowa in its support of third parties which adhered to "cheap money" policies. General James B. Weaver, Iowa's own Greenbacker, ran in 1880 as that party's nominee for President.[4] In 1884, the

INTRODUCTION
— 5 —

Iowa Greenbackers combined with the Democrats and produced four congressional victories as well as a narrow loss in the race for the governorship.

The People's Party—most popular in wheat states plagued by oscillating market prices—received relatively weak support from corn-growing Iowa. But the state nevertheless provided important leadership to the Populist crusade. In 1892, General Weaver ran again for president, this time as the Populist candidate appealing to those who were victims of "tariffs, railroads, middlemen, speculators, warehousers, and monopolistic producers of farm equipment."[5] He collected 22 electoral votes in the nation but received only 5% of Iowa's presidential vote.[6] Four years later, as the Populists fused with the Democratic Party, Iowa Governor and Republican-turned-Democrat Horace Boies nearly grasped that party's nomination for the presidency, only to have it swept from his reach at the national convention by the silver-tongued oratory of William Jennings Bryan, who delivered his electrifying "Cross of Gold" speech.

Despite the progressive efforts of Governor William Larrabee and the third parties, as Iowa closed its frontier era and advanced into the 1900s, a preponderant railroad-business coalition remained the best organized and most potent political force in the state. Neither the discredited Democratic Party nor the fringe third party movements could provide a strong base for a permanent reform movement. But the inherited strains of reform were not lost. Instead, battles between "progressives" and "standpatters" ensued within the Republican Party itself. One historian has defined the contrast between these two groups in this way:

Progressives wanted tariff reform downward and they wanted reciprocity; they wanted legislation to curb the great business interests, especially

A PARTY REBORN
— 6 —

to guard against the formation of trusts with monopolistic power; they wanted regulation of the railroads, the grain elevator companies, the insurance companies, the meat-packing companies, the stock market ("Wall Street"); they wanted reforms to wipe out "the shame of the cities," and they wanted more democracy in state government, hence their support of the direct primary, the initiative and referendum, and the recall. Standpatters opposed some or all of these objectives, in varying degrees.[7]

Iowa produced a succession of brilliant and outspoken progressive Republican leaders. Albert Baird Cummins, a friend of Larrabee, served as governor from 1903 to 1907, and advocated widespread reforms: increasing railroad taxes, licensing and examining insurance companies, and legislating pure food and drug and direct-primary voting laws. Following the death of Senator William Boyd Allison, Cummins left the governor's chair to join Jonathan P. Dolliver in the Senate, where the two Republicans served as powerful spokesmen for progressive policies. Pushing for conservation, national railroad regulation, and tariff reform, the two, along with Robert M. La Follette of Wisconsin, helped to spearhead progressive insurgency in the United States Senate. When, for example, President William H. Taft called for tariff reforms, but then, in 1909, allowed Congressman Sereno E. Payne (New York) and Senator Nelson W. Aldrich (Rhode Island) to emasculate the bill with innumerable amendments, Dolliver and Cummins alerted the nation with their vociferous objections to the President's lack of commitment to progressive ideals.

Although the progressive lights of the nation dimmed as America entered World War I, Iowa's trend of sending its bright radical stars to the Senate continued. Smith W. Brookhart of Washington, Iowa, a wealthy man who considered even Senator Cummins too conservative, challenged the incumbent Cummins twice, beating him the se-

INTRODUCTION

cond time, in 1926. Once in the Senate himself, Brookhart assailed the conservative policies of the Coolidge Administration. As author Joseph Frazier Wall describes: "So in the midst of Coolidge conservatism, Iowa elected the most radical senator in its history, a man who had denounced his own party leadership and had refused to support Coolidge in 1924, a man who openly advocated public ownership of railroads and utilities, direct federal aid to farmers, and the unionization of labor."[8]

In the years of farm depression that followed the war, a brief new wave of agrarian radicalism arose from a curious mixture of right- and left-wing impulses. In the United States House of Representatives, Iowa Congressman Gilbert N. Haugen co-sponsored the McNary-Haugen bills, which sought to establish a two-tier pricing system for agricultural export commodities. This marked the first important instance in which progressives addressed themselves to a specifically agricultural problem.[9] In northwest Iowa, farmer Milo Reno pleaded forcefully with the federal government to guarantee price supports for farmers as members of his own Farmers' Holiday Association violently protested insufferably low market prices. Then he flirted with extremists on both ends of the political spectrum, including Huey Long and Father Charles E. Coughlin, to oppose the policies of President Franklin Delano Roosevelt.

The New Deal years transformed the political allegiances of much of the rest of the nation, but Iowa voters did not reward Democrats with elective offices except in the worst Depression years. Iowa Democrats won by landslide margins in 1932, 1934, and 1936, but by 1938 farm prices had started to recover and Republicans recaptured much of their traditional strength. Except for the surprising Iowa victory in 1948 of Harry S. Truman, joined in triumph by Guy M. Gillette in his bid for the U.S. Senate that same

A PARTY REBORN

year, the GOP won steadily in the war years, much as they had since the Civil War.

In the decades after World War II, Iowa experienced an agricultural and technological revolution that spurred rapid urbanization and industrialization. From their urban homes, farmers who had moved to the city now voiced their new needs to state legislators; but such demands fell largely upon the inattentive ears of rural members who completely controlled the malapportioned General Assembly. The railroad hegemony had long since dissolved, but now powerful rural and small-town interest groups dominated both the Republican Party and the Iowa legislature. In the largest cities Democrats now outnumbered their GOP neighbors, yet they lacked effective means to translate their majority into power. Gradually, however, restless party leaders in cities such as Des Moines stirred the ambitions of party workers and created new designs for political victory.

It was within this political framework that the Democratic Party of Iowa forcefully re-emerged in the 1960s. Democrat Harold E. Hughes began the process, leading Iowans from their rural past to a new era that held rural, small town and urban interests in tenuous balance. Hughes did not limit himself to Iowa issues alone. As governor and then as United States Senator, Hughes confronted head-on the nation's most controversial cultural issues of the day. He called Iowans to alarm — not to arms — when America became embroiled in a tragic war in Vietnam. Hughes encouraged others to follow his progressive lead in helping to end the fighting in Vietnam and to change Iowa laws. He fought for reforms within the Democratic Party so that those other voices might be heard. Himself a lay preacher, Hughes employed a moralistic fervor as had the Populists and progressives before him in Iowa history, seeking to les-

INTRODUCTION

sen special interest powers by increasing direct democracy in Iowa government, in the Democratic Party, and in the corridors of the United States Capitol.

It would be inaccurate to attribute this striking era of political change between 1950 and 1974 simply to the coincidence of charismatic leadership offered in a time of confusing social circumstances. Indeed, Iowa's progressive surge, marked by the successes of Hughes and the rise of the Democratic Party, resonated with energies derived from progressive traditions as old as the state itself. Also crucial to sustained Democratic successes was the building of the party organization. Behind Hughes, a new generation of Democratic politicians came to the forefront in the early 1970s; men like John C. Culver and Dick Clark shared Hughes's ideals but also brought with them an intense desire to establish a grassroots political structure across the state. With hard work, competent leadership, and effective organization of good party machinery, in 1974 the Democratic Party was Iowa's dominant political party. The Democrats now gave expression to the state's progressive instincts in what had become an extremely competitive two-party system.

Iowa Democratic Party Chairman Jake More
DES MOINES REGISTER

II

URBANIZATION AND THE SILENT DEMOCRATS

A PERCEPTIVE OBSERVER describing the political atmosphere of Iowa in 1948 might well have said that state politics entered a new period of consensus after World War II. Interest groups that before the War had fractured into various combinations of battling coalitions now joined to endorse the same Republican candidate for governor in the GOP primary election and, later, in the general election.

Only one year earlier, in 1947, two of the most powerful of these interest groups had merged forces in bitter conflict with the state's rising labor organizations. One of the groups, the Iowa Manufacturers Association (IMA), was loosely structured, but its leaders had access to great industrial wealth and were able politicians, people who could effectively lobby for the legislation they helped to design. At the same time, over 100,000 farmers were voicing their anti-labor union sentiments through the fastest growing and best organized interest group in the state: the Iowa Farm Bureau Federation (IFBF). And when these two groups combined their efforts, they successfully rammed stringent anti-labor laws through the legislature over the vociferous objections of the state's major labor organizations.

By contrast, in 1948 the 100,000-member Iowa Federation of Labor and the more than 25,000-member Congress of Industrial Organizations that had fought so hard against

A PARTY REBORN
— 12 —

the IMA and the IFBF over the labor laws now joined them to support Republican William Beardsley in his race for the governorship. Iowa politics, it seemed, had moved into an era of unanimity and stability.[1]

In 1958, however, almost any observer would have clearly seen that these earlier joint endorsements of a single gubernatorial candidate reflected an illusory and impermanent accord. In the intervening decade the major labor organizations in the state had publicly switched their allegiances from the GOP to the Democratic Party. The Democrats, long dormant as a real political force, had themselves been jarred awake by some surprising victories and by the overthrow of entrenched party leaders. Soon, by the early 1960s, the entire state would become embroiled in fiercely contested battles between parties, interest groups, and private citizens—battles over issues scarcely discussed ten years earlier.

THE ORGANIZATIONAL STRENGTH of Iowa's Democratic Party in 1948 was probably no greater than it had been in 1940 when, at the request of former Democratic Governor Clyde L. Herring, Shelby County lawyer Jake More had first become state chairman. More, an energetic and personable chairman, had attempted to build a party structure based on political patronage. In the 1940s, many federal positions were distributed through patronage, and More developed a cadre of county chairmen who attempted to elicit political contributions from those who had received Post Office, Census Bureau, Agriculture Department, or other federal appointments from the Truman Administration. Postmasters, for example, were expected to contribute five to ten dollars each month to Democratic Party coffers. By adding these patronage donations to money raised at fundraising dinners, the unsalaried More was barely able

SILENT DEMOCRATS

to cover the biennial expenditures of over $50,000 for the various activities and campaigns of Iowa Democrats.[2]

More worked hard at his job. A superb hotel lobby politician, he maintained close ties to virtually all political factions of both parties. Nevertheless, with More as the Democratic state chairman, Republicans rested easy, content that there would be no serious challenges to their incumbencies. They were right. Throughout the 1940s the Republicans effectively silenced Chairman More's Democrats, who failed to gain political offices.

Three primary reasons explain why Jake More's Democratic Party produced so few successes. First, the party depended upon the purse strings of patronage for its economic sustenance, and partisan loyalties, so generated, tended to stagnate and disintegrate. Donald J. Mitchell, who served as national committeeman for the Iowa Democrats from 1953 to 1968, once analyzed the weaknesses of the federal patronage system:

> I have seen many instances where a local organization, speaking of course from the political viewpoint, has been torn asunder by a very desirable appointment to a rural route or to a post office vacancy where half a dozen people are contending for the same.
>
> ...I think in the main, these appointments are divisive rather than beneficial to our Party. The sad fact about this patronage is once the person has been appointed and qualified under the permanent Civil Service, he becomes somewhat useless to the Party. Very few of the appointees continue any political interest whatsoever, and very few of them pay any obligation to the Party.[3]

Second, Jake More and his fellow Democrats lacked an historical tradition and a knowledge about organizational politics. As early as the end of the 19th Century other midwestern states had seen the rise of Democratic political machines in urban areas, but no parallel development occurred in Iowa. Instead, during that period—a time of great population growth in Iowa—waves of foreign and

A PARTY REBORN
– 14 –

American immigrants who arrived in the state quickly dispersed to many attractive and available rural areas. This scattering prevented the sudden burdensome increases in city populations that elsewhere gave rise to political machines. In addition, Iowa Democrats under Jake More remained oblivious to organizational methods that might easily have increased Democratic vote totals in urban areas. The chairman habitually launched "get out the vote" drives consisting of an impotent arsenal of press releases and newspaper advertisements.[4]

A third reason for the scarcity of Democratic triumphs in the Jake More years, many believed, was that More personally enjoyed more power and prestige with no elected officials of his own party serving above him to interfere with his wishes. If the Democratic Party swept the presidential elections, for instance, and there were no Democrats from his state in a major office, the power of the patronage appointments fell directly into the hands of Jake More. In addition, if national political figures came to the state and there were no Democratic office holders available to greet them appropriately, the duty fell to the party chairman alone.

Of course, it would be unfair to blame all Democratic failures on Jake More. In fact, More consistently denied that his own desires for patronage powers contributed to Democratic Party defeats. Rather, alleged More, the stigma of past defeats and the low incomes paid to elected officials prevented strong and attractive Democrats from pursuing public careers. "We worked to get lots of good candidates," said More. "Of course people didn't think Democrats could win, and the offices didn't pay very well. It was hard in those days to go full time in politics. Successful businessmen were reluctant to run and lose control of their businesses and become openly political for the

SILENT DEMOCRATS

Democrats. Unsuccessful people were always willing to run, but we didn't want to have them on our ticket."[5]

Senator Guy M. Gillette's campaign victory in 1948 allowed More his only notable success. Given such a string of defeats, it seems, the Chairman should have been easy prey for an ouster. However, opposition to him was stymied for years when his own considerable political skills combined with a critical event in 1948 to fix him securely in the state chair. More recalls:

> Some say Harry Truman got his campaign off the ground here at Dexter when Herb Plambeck organized an event [the National Plowing Match, September 28, 1948] and over 100,000 persons came to see Truman. I've never seen anything like it: people were standing shoulder to shoulder and could hardly move. I know Truman complained after it was all over, because I had made him get on the train at Davenport and travel clear across the state to Dexter. When he got back to Kansas City, he told the national Democratic Chairman, "That damned Jake More! He treated me like a candidate for County Sheriff and made me stop at every little town along the way!" Well, he may have been mad, but, as I say, the Dexter thing was spectacular and it really got Harry off on a good start. During the course of the campaign he and I became very good friends, and I continued to see him often after he left office. He came to Iowa to make several speeches at my request.[6]

Although being labelled a "Democrat" in Iowa in the 1950s did not lend prestige to many people, few politicians in either party gained the status Jake More garnered through this special relationship with Harry Truman which began in 1948. Because no state Democrat could match the fame or influence of More, the Democratic Party of Iowa remained in his control for ten years thereafter. The party built its power structure on the sands of patronage appointments; it was incapable of presenting strong opposition to the candidates of the Republican Party.

Thus, it would seem that one of the most important explanations for Iowa's apparent consensus of 1948 was that the state Democratic Party did not provide a viable alternative to the GOP. The Democrats could not create the political base they needed to attract the support of certain interest groups. If Iowa's labor unions, for instance, had aligned with the Democratic Party in 1948, they would have only sapped their already limited strength by lessening their access to influential people of whom the Republican Party boasted many and the Democratic Party but few.

In one important respect the Republican Party resembled the Democratic Party. Both were decentralized organizations, unable to formulate aggressive party policies. But unlike the party structure of the Democrats, which seemed devoid of widespread allegiances, the GOP organization was alive with vital internal competition which accompanied political victory and power. Whereas continual defeat forced Jake More and his friends in the 1940s and 1950s to play the role of political outsiders, Republican leaders found themselves preoccupied with efforts to accommodate the conflicts of those interest groups vying for influence beneath the straining fabric of the party's ideological canopy.

Of course, the domination of state politics and of the Republican Party by special interests was not new to Iowa. After the railroad barons of the 19th and early 20th centuries lost their grip on the party, new groups like the Iowa bankers arose to fill the political vacuum. When the Depression broke the power of the bankers (which, in any case, had never matched the earlier power of the railroad magnates), the Iowa Manufacturers Association, and a little later, the Iowa Farm Bureau Federation emerged as the most powerful organizations in the state. Even though they were not allied with each other in all legislative battles, a shared conservative economic philosophy and a common antipathy towards the labor unions encouraged the two

SILENT DEMOCRATS
— 17 —

groups to cooperate in the most important postwar confrontations.

Both the IMA and the IFBF exerted great influence in Iowa politics, but they acquired that influence through markedly different means. On the one hand, the IMA was not organized on a county or a community basis. It was composed instead of approximately 500 manufacturing members, and it spent large sums of money to alter public opinion on various issues through media campaigns. No lobbyist in the State Capitol was more effective than IMA director Ed Kimball. Shortly after the close of the war, when the IMA clout had grown to its greatest proportions, wry legislative observers noted that "when Ed Kimball took snuff, the Governor sneezed."[7] For years, the IMA's influence was partly responsible for the anti-union and anti-corporation tax sentiments (among others) of the state's citizens and government officials.[8]

On the other hand, the IFBF consolidated its power by building grassroots organizations in all 99 Iowa counties. Founded in 1919 as a national group, state Farm Bureau organizations in many states — but especially in Iowa — had formed symbiotic relationships with the Extension Service of the federal Agriculture Department. As stipulated in the Smith-Lever Act of 1914, the purpose of the Extension Service was to diffuse ". . . among the people of the United States useful and practical information on subjects relating to agriculture and home economics and to encourage the application of the same."[9] The focal points of the Extension Service organization were the county agents; in Iowa at least, every county supported such an agent, who served as teacher and advisor to farmers and others interested in agriculture.

In order to receive federal monies from the Extension Service, funds which were in fact distributed through state

A PARTY REBORN
— 18 —

government, local citizens in each county had to provide matching funds. To provide the organized basis of support needed for the Extension Service agent, the Farm Bureaus of Iowa and the other states were created. The relationship of the Farm Bureau to the Extension Service was particularly strong in Iowa, where the IFBF acted as the Extension sponsor in every county. Often housed in the very same county buildings, the IFBF acted in concert with Extension Service agents across the state for over 30 years. So close did the relationship become that in 1955 Secretary of Agriculture Ezra Taft Benson delivered an edict requiring the ties between the two be officially severed.[10]

By the end of World War II, the IFBF's annual membership had grown to an average of well over 100,000 (one membership per family), making it by far the largest pressure group in the state and the second largest Farm Bureau organization in the nation. When the shrewd and energetic Kenneth Thatcher, armed with an annual budget approaching a million dollars, became its executive secretary and director in 1948, the IFBF quickly reinforced its 100 field offices and doubled the size of its lobbying team and staff. Even after Secretary Benson forcibly separated the IFBF and the Extension Service, the IFBF retained its own strong county-by-county organization.[11]

"The Farm Bureau has never had power," Thatcher once demurred. "We have had influence." But with this "influence," the IFBF soon surpassed the IMA to become the premier power broker in the Republican Party and, therefore, in Iowa politics. The ease and speed with which the IFBF gathered this strength can be attributed to the lack of a central, controlling entity within the Republican Party. GOP power was dispersed among the state's localities and counties, where well-established interest groups accumulated it for their own uses. Virtually assured

SILENT DEMOCRATS
— 19 —

of success in most general elections until the 1960s, Republicans often fought heated battles in the party's primaries. The IFBF actively encouraged its members to attend precinct caucuses and county meetings, and many of those attending were themselves nominated for various elective positions. After the primaries, when the Republican and Democratic candidates had been selected, the IFBF held "know your candidates" meetings where its members implicitly endorsed particular candidates. The organization subsequently supported these candidates politically and—sometimes—financially. The organizational efforts of the IFBF paid off. By 1959, all major committees of Iowa's General Assembly (in fact, all House committees) were chaired by persons who openly claimed IFBF membership.[12]

The IMA and the IFBF left little room for other interest groups to maneuver. But the 1940s and 1950s were the years when Iowa's labor unions began to appear as powers in their own right. It was difficult to assess the exact size of labor's membership by the 1950s. Union leaders estimated the state's Federation of Labor (AFL) to have had between 60,000 and 75,000 members, whereas perhaps 40,000 Iowans paid dues to the various locals of the Congress of Industrial Organizations (CIO).[13] The unions did not at first gain political powers commensurate with their growth. Therefore, they were unable seriously to challenge the IMA or IFBF.

The lack of internal organization impeded labor's effective political expression in state politics. For example, often crippled by its own federated structure and unable to act promptly, the Iowa AFL generally subscribed to political creeds that emphasized local, rather than state or national, activism. Only 30% of local members paid dues to the state organization, which was divided into 19 separate central labor bodies. AFL leaders often ignored issues that extended beyond the city limits of their own communities.[14]

In contrast, the CIO, spearheaded by the leaders of the 9,000-strong United Auto Workers, grew ambitious for political power. CIO leaders were outspoken in their demands for revisions of various labor-related laws, but the CIO lacked sufficient numbers and a wide enough geographical distribution (its 100 locals were primarily in the eastern, urban part of the state) to make enough legislators wary of their clout.[15]

To a large extent, the differences between the efforts of Iowa's AFL and CIO reflected the greater fissure that until 1956 split their national counterparts. As a result, not only were the internal structures of the major labor organizations in disarray, but so too were their relations with each other.[16] In the 1950 Democratic primary for United States Senator, Iowa's AFL and CIO backed opposing candidates.

Other special interest groups vied for political influence with the dominant Republicans, but they tended to be concerned with narrow rather than broad issues. Therefore, they did not often attempt to arm wrestle with their more powerful adversaries—the labor groups, the IFBF, and the IMA. Lobbyists for groups like the Iowa State Education Association, the Iowa Bar Association, the Iowa Medical Society, and the Associated General Contractors of Iowa remained preoccupied primarily with legislation directly related to the activities of their own groups.

Consequently, in the decade following World War II dominant interest groups in Iowa competed for power largely within the loosely structured confines of the Republican Party. The Democrats did not seek office aggressively or successfully. The GOP remained the only party in which

SILENT DEMOCRATS

individuals or groups could hope to satisfy political needs. Organizations like the IMA and IFBF, with access both to financial resources and to able leadership, easily accumulated powers of their own and effectively guided Republican Party policies and, in effect, the General Assembly.[17] Such an interest hegemony could have continued for many decades—like the earlier hegemony of the railroad barons and the bankers—had it not been for a dramatic transformation of Iowa's social character. An agricultural and manufacturing revolution prompted rapid urbanization and altered the very consciousness of the state at such an explosive rate that this old structure of power rapidly crumbled. In the twenty years after 1950, new powers arose and began to reconstruct the political order.

FROM 1940 TO 1970 new economic forces brought about significant changes in the lives and perceptions of Iowans. In the previous half-century, from 1890 to 1940, only gradual increases in population, urbanization, and industrialization had transpired. These increases had been so slight that they clearly distinguished the state from the rest of the nation. While the population of the country had doubled, Iowa's population increased by less than one-third, particularly because many young people left the state to seek their fortune elsewhere. The expanding industries in other parts of the nation acted as social magnets, drawing rural dwellers to urban centers. But in Iowa no great urban-industrial areas had developed to attract farmers and small-town residents who chose to remain in their state.

Between 1940 and 1970, however, labor shortages and increased agricultural demands generated by World War II and its aftermath altered the state's demography. New in-

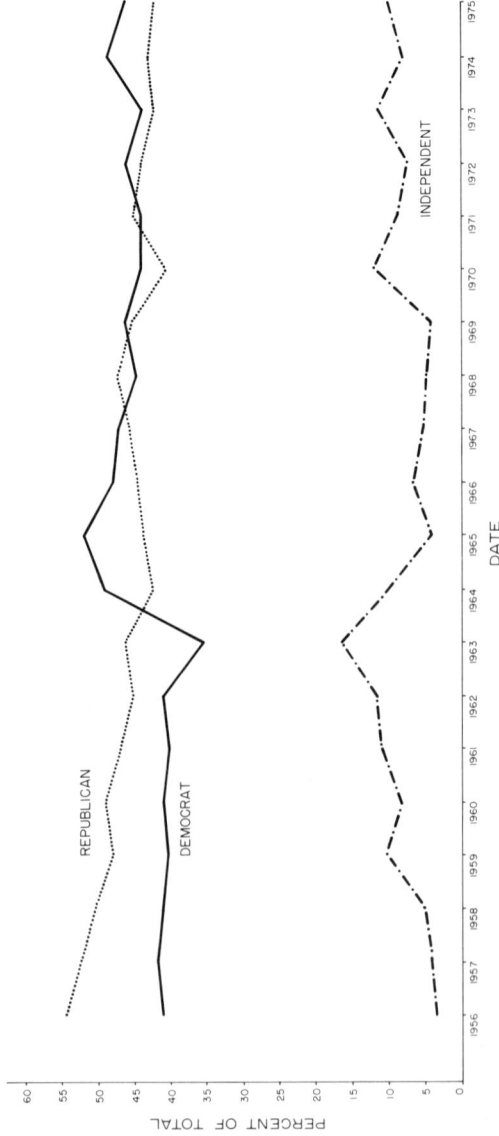

Figure 1. Partisan Preference of Iowa Voters, 1956-1975

Source: Summary of the Iowa Poll provided by the *Des Moines Register and Tribune*. For the same data in tabular form, see Chapter 4, note 42.

ventions permanently changed the habits of centuries. As an occupation, farming developed from a labor-intensive into an energy- and capital-intensive endeavor. Roswell Garst, an Iowa farmer, promoter of hybrid seed corn, and advocate of innovative farming methods, stood at the vortex of this revolution in agricultural production. A unique witness to its impact, he observed:

> When the state was founded, it was said it took an hour of a man's time to make a bushel of corn. By 1940, it took less than four minutes to make that same bushel, and in the 1970s the figure is well under two minutes and the basket is now filled with hybrid corn. The time is less now because hybridization, fertilization, and a new breed of machinery have increased the yield. In the 1930s the U.S. raised more than 100 million acres of corn, with the average yield of 21 bushels per acre. Now, we raise corn on only about 60 million acres, but the national average is over 80 bushels—over 100 bushels in Iowa—from every acre we plant, or over a four-fold increase.[18]

As Iowans abandoned the old labor-intensive practices for more economically efficient methods that produced grand new agricultural surpluses, the need for human labor on farms diminished. Farms increased in size dramatically. Tens of thousands of farmhouse hearths stood deserted when their inhabitants were forced to find work elsewhere.[19]

From 1940 to 1970 considerable redistribution of Iowa's population took place (see Figure 2). In 1900, slightly less than one-fourth of the state's citizens had lived in towns of more than 2,500, and by 1940 still only about 40% resided in larger communities. But as the *Des Moines Sunday Register* noted, World War II had increased the pace of change:

> Between 1940 and 1950, the larger centers in Iowa almost without exception gained in population. The rural areas and the small towns lost. The war was a major factor in the population shift. High wages and good working conditions in war plants attracted thousands of rural people to

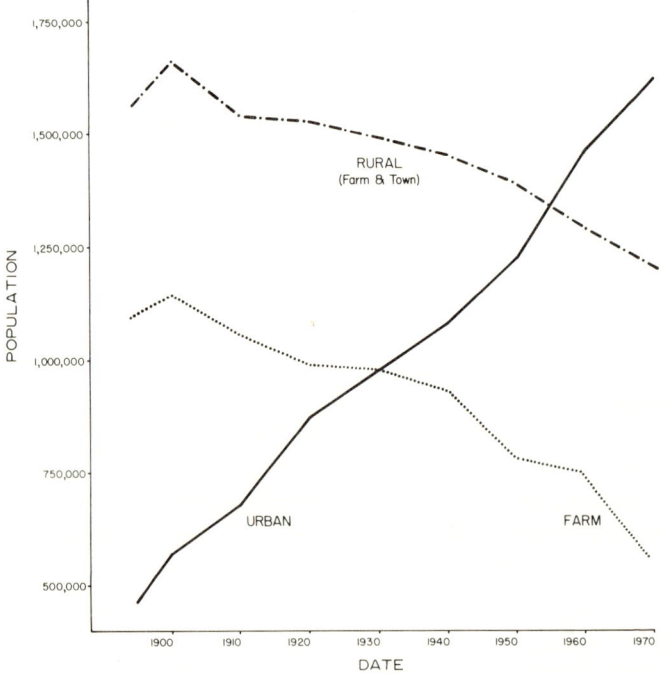

Figure 2. Urban-Rural Trends in Iowa, 1900-1970

Source: U.S. Department of Commerce, Bureau of the Census, *Eighteenth Census of the United States,* volume 1, *Population,* part 14 (Washington, D.C., 1962); idem., *Nineteenth Census of the United States,* volume 1, *Population,* part 17 (Washington, D.C., 1973); idem., *Historical Statistics of the United States: Colonial Times to 1970,* part 1 (Washington, D.C., 1975), p. 458.

the cities, both inside Iowa and in other states. Most of the migration was permanent. Also, many of the farm youths who served in the armed forces haven't returned to the farm to live.[20]

The population shift combined the exodus of the young (at a rate of nearly 27,000 per year) and the urbanization of the middle-aged. In 1960, the U.S. Census Bureau would reveal that Iowa, for the first time in its history, had more citizens living in urban than in rural areas. Also, that same census was to report that the average Iowan was older than the average inhabitant of any other state in the nation. These trends were to continue. By the 1970s, 57.2% of Iowans would reside in urban areas, and only Florida would claim a higher percentage of older persons.[21]

Given the strength of the urbanization momentum perhaps the most unusual characteristic of the state's population base was the large proportion of medium-sized communities that remained intact even as residents of neighboring rural areas brushed by on their way to Iowa's suburbs and cities, or out of the state completely.[22] For example, from 1930 to 1960 Iowa towns ranging in population size from 500 to 2,499 held nearly constant in total numbers, while the number of those with more than 2,500 dwellers increased steadily and those with under 500 diminished.[23] As towns died, new ones arose in other parts of the state. In particular, "dormitory towns" adjacent to metropolitan areas — places where people could live cheaply and yet enjoy the amenities of urban life — prospered. Thus, Iowa was witnessing a striking constancy in both the quantity of its communities of moderate size and the number of people who lived in them. A significant qualitative change was also occurring in the nature and the location of some of these towns. More small towns were now directly dependent upon the urban centers for their survival.

A PARTY REBORN
— 26 —

Another prominent feature of the state's population shift was that the southwest quadrant of Iowa emptied as the eastern and central regions filled. The presence of consistently fertile farm soils and the proximity of the state's east-central areas to the industrial centers of the Great Lakes and Mississippi River industrial belts greatly aided their growth. Conversely, southwest Iowa provided proportionately fewer economic opportunities than it had earlier in the 20th Century. In fact, from 1940 to 1960, the population of the congressional district in this portion of the state had one of the five most rapidly declining populations in the entire nation. During that period three-fourths of all its urban communities lost residents.[24]

An initially less perceptible yet more dynamic expansion of industrial and manufacturing capabilities accompanied the exponential increases in farm productivity and brisk population redistribution. Between 1939 and 1947, manufacturing employment in the state increased by 59% compared to a national growth rate of 50%. In 1949, for the first time, the gross industrial product of Iowa equaled the value of the agricultural goods it produced. Ten years later the value of Iowa's industrial output had grown to exceed that of farming by a ratio of 2.5:1. By 1970, the ratio had again doubled.[25]

Unlike the adjacent states of Illinois and Missouri, Iowa's new industries did not concentrate in one or two large metropolitan areas. Instead, the fifteen largest cities, sharing over 50% of the state's population, also shared Iowa's manufacturing plants. From the ever larger, ever more mechanized farms which lay between these growing cities, many farmers would themselves drive to the cities to work in factories when their intensively fertilized crops matured and their mammoth implements rested. By 1959, no less than 14% of Iowa farmers worked 100 days or

SILENT DEMOCRATS
— 27 —

more away from their farms. In such counties as Wapello (whose largest city was Ottumwa) and Polk (Des Moines), the figure exceeded 35%.[26] Even the state's rural residents, it seemed, were becoming urbanized.

Given the magnitude of Iowa's postwar economic and social transformations, it is perhaps not surprising that the concerns and perceptions of the state's citizens were altered as well. Indeed, by 1973 the era of "farm consciousness" had given way to a new era of "consumer consciousness" among urban dwellers. In that year, a public opinion poll reportedly indicated that the typical housewife in Des Moines was no more sympathetic to, or understanding of, a farmer's problems than were the housewives of New York City.[27] This change helped to produce a re-alignment of Iowa's political forces, converting Iowa from a "one-party Republican" to a "two-party competitive" state.[28]

After 1940, Iowa voters clustered into three general categories: a politically volatile farm population; a largely Republican constituency living in smaller communities; and an urban population oriented towards the Democratic Party. Farmers, though a steadily declining proportion of Iowa's population, maintained their heritage of political independence, continuing to vacillate in their support of particular parties. Though they became more Democratic since the New Deal offered farmers much-needed relief legislation during the Depression, market prices strongly swayed their political choices.

In smaller towns of less than 10,000, people seldom budged from their Republican loyalties.[29] The more conservative tendencies and slogans of the Republican Party remained popular among those whose lives were tethered to the small businesses of Main Street and the potluck dinners of church basements.

In urban centers of more than 10,000 people, the relationship between urbanization and an increased preference for the Democratic Party became strong. Several factors explain this trend.[30] Larger cities supported major industries and manufacturing plants. Their residents had greater needs for social services than those who lived in smaller communities. The anti-government, individualistic focus of the conservative Republicans became unattractive to new urban dwellers.

Another reason why urban dwellers severed their traditional Republican ties may have been their sense of fracture—feelings created, in part, when people nurtured by the closely knit community of small towns confronted the coldness and the more glaring class divisions characteristic of larger cities. Ruth Suckow, the Iowa novelist, writing of her childhood experiences long before the state's modern social and economic revolution took place, expressed her emotional response to her own family's move from small-town Hawarden to an Iowa urban center:

The social and economic boundaries of church membership, especially in country towns (and almost all Iowa towns, large or small, are in some degree country or agricultural towns) were quite wide apart: they took in bankers and day laborers....Our parsonage was far from being a developing ground for any hard-and-fast divisions of humankind, the saved and the unsaved, the elect and the damned, the powerful and "successful" and the unimportant. All entered it on essentially the same human footing....

[And after moving to a larger city] I remember our embarrassment and inward seething when we were "briefed," as one might say, by a young woman acquaintance on the occasion of our father's assuming the pastorate of what was called in Iowa a city church: as to our manners, and the correct dress for Sunday services—we must always be sure to wear white gloves for Sunday, white kid in the winter and silk in summer—and particularly as to those who were and those who were not the right people to cultivate among the church members. The young woman supposed that she was doing us a kindness, and that since we had been living in a town of only six thousand population, as opposed to sixty thousand, such advice would be needed.[31]

SILENT DEMOCRATS
— 29 —

Like Ruth Suckow before them, thousands of Iowans in the decades following World War II moved from their farms and small-town homes to residences in larger cities, where few churches now served as the schools of democracy. It is not difficult to imagine that, for many of them, profound feelings of personal dislocation—perhaps even "seethings"—accompanied such moves and may have affected their political attitudes.

Indeed, when major demographic factors are considered, only urbanization provides important clues as to why Iowa witnessed an increasing preference for the Democratic Party during the postwar decades. There is a consistent lack of statistical significance in the relationships between the voting behavior of citizens and their education levels, incomes, or ages.[32]

If in demographic terms only urbanization seems an important influence, there were other factors not so easily measured by quantitative techniques that also played a prominent role in the transformation of political attitudes. Emerging issues, invigorated organizational efforts, and the strong personalities of the candidates themselves became important in altering the choices of Iowa voters.

IOWA POLITICS in the immediate postwar years had been dominated by competition for power among various interest groups within the loosely structured confines of the Republican Party. As a result, Republican Party leaders for many years were reduced to the role of officiators. Then, as the social and economic infrastructure of the state altered, new and potent issues came forth manifesting the social changes. In the political debates and legislative struggles that followed, the disproportionate power the rurally oriented special interests had accumulated was, for the first time, overtly displayed to the state's urban citizens. Among the most salient of the issues under debate were the shifting tax burden and its impact on school redistricting and financing, road use taxes and county government costs, "liquor-by-the-drink," labor laws, and, most crucially, legislative reapportionment.

By the 1950s, Iowans paid combined state income and sales taxes somewhat below the per capita U.S. average, but they paid local property taxes close to the highest in the country. When the three taxes were summed, Iowans felt themselves unduly burdened by their tax load. One cause of the increasingly high taxes was that Iowans traditionally spent large sums upon secondary roads, education, and county governments. The state had taken pride in its rural roads, among the best in the nation, and in its literacy rate, unmatched by any other state. But as the population base shifted, the tax formulas did not alter correspondingly. State legislators, influenced by the IMA and IFBF and over the objections of urban groups, continued to spend disproportionately large amounts on rural projects. As a result, city residents paid taxes both to maintain rural roads while their own streets decayed and to finance the many small and costly school districts of the townships while their own children attended larger, more economical schools.[33]

The "liquor-by-the-drink" issue was primarily an urban phenomenon. It arose when a mounting number of Iowans protested the stringent laws of 1934 prohibiting the sale of hard liquors "over the counter" in bars and clubs.[34] Liquor could be purchased only in state-owned stores, but Iowans did not modify their drinking habits in response to the law. All of the neighboring states had less severe liquor laws, and Iowans readily crossed state borders to purchase and drink liquor. Six of the state's seven largest cities were located near its borders, and businessmen argued that

Iowa lost business revenues because of the state's strict statute. Other urban interests generally opposed the law. Many pointed out that the law, initially written and now kept in the State Code by rural interests, encouraged hypocrisy. Thousands of "key clubs," established to circumvent possible prosecution of the law by disguising as "service clubs," collected dues from their members and served liquor just as bars in nearby states did. Legal action against those groups which existed only for drinking would have jeopardized the many legitimate fraternal and service organizations in the state. The liquor question provided a potentially divisive issue for politicians.

In addition to taxes and alcohol, other vital postwar controversies centered on the writing of new state labor laws. In 1946, an unprecedented number of strikes broke out across the nation in response to the difficult adjustments of peacetime. In June, Congress passed the Taft-Hartley Act, establishing new legal restrictions upon union organizing. Section 14-B of the Act made illegal "closed shop" agreements, but stipulated that "union shops" could be organized. In the union shop anyone working for that shop must join the appropriate union and pay dues after being hired; the now illegal closed shop agreement would have required workers to join the designated unions before being considered for employment.

In Iowa, newspaper accounts of labor strikes and union corruption in the East prompted legislators to put restrictions on union power extending beyond the guidelines of the Taft-Hartley Act. The state joined other southern, midwestern, and western states with various versions of the "right-to-work" laws, which sought to ban union shop agreements. Over the vehement objections of urban Democrats — and of liberal Republicans in the General Assembly who feared permanent alienation of labor members

A PARTY REBORN
— 32 —

from the GOP—the IMA and the IFBF rallied their rural and small-town forces in 1947 to write perhaps the two most rigorous right-to-work laws in the nation.[35] The first prohibited the union shop, but it also forbade employers from deducting union dues from an employee's paycheck without the written consent of both the employee and the employee's spouse. The second law sharply limited the legal means by which unions in the state could call strikes.[36] On April 28, 1947, Iowa became the ninth of what would be nineteen states to enact right-to-work laws. As Republican Governor Robert Blue signed the bill into law, 50,000 laborers demonstrated in protest outside the Capitol.[37]

Protests against the labor laws and against the state tax formulas came with increasing force from urban areas during the 1940s and 1950s, but the General Assemblies of this period regularly ignored these and other urban demands because legislative seats were allocated distinctly in favor of the rural counties. Understandably, reapportionment rose to the surface as the most important and hotly contested issue in a half-century of Iowa politics.

The writers of the 1857 Constitution of Iowa had expressed a Jeffersonian idealism that envisioned each generation as capable of adapting itself to new conditions. The political leaders of that time provided future citizens with two reapportionment alternatives: either through the joint actions of two consecutive Assemblies or through the efforts of a state-wide constitutional convention to be held by referendum once per decade. In the years immediately following the Civil War, General Assemblies regularly redrew district boundaries to correspond to changing demographic patterns.

In 1904, however, and again in 1928, rural forces prompted the state to alter the original Constitution's

SILENT DEMOCRATS
— 33 —

provisions for reapportionment. The 1904 amendment required that each county, regardless of population size, would be guaranteed at least one House member and that the nine most populous counties would be allotted two representatives. The amendment of 1928 changed the composition of the Senate, also to the advantage of rural citizens. It directed that no county could be represented by more than one senator, a provision giving the most sparsely inhabited counties proportionally far greater representation than the most densely populated ones. In effect, legislative seats were no longer assigned according to population, but according to land areas. No further reapportionments were undertaken.[38] By the 1950s, one-fourth of the state's citizens (most of them rural) elected a majority of the House, and about one-third of the voters elected a majority of the Senate. Indeed, in the fifty years following the 1904 amendment, Iowa had created its own system of "rotten boroughs," and justice was lost in the allocation of legislative seats. As the *Des Moines Register* acknowledged: "Residents of Iowa small towns and rural counties who have long since died or moved away carry more weight in the legislature than the swelling populations of the growing industrial cities. Legislators who represent more ghosts than men are elected on the same ticket with unnecessary county elective officials and play ball with them on county roads. They play ball with ghost inhabitants of shrunken school districts on school reorganization."[39]

Throughout the 1950s the state conventions of both political parties discussed and debated the new cluster of urban issues. At their conventions, both parties recommended action on reapportionment, but seldom did a General Assembly act on these recommendations. Many urban Republicans attempted to battle the organized rural and

A PARTY REBORN

small-town interests within their own party but without any real success. Even though two-thirds of the state's citizens openly favored reapportionment[40] of legislative seats as a means to distribute political power equitably, year after year groups like the IMA and IFBF blocked all such attempts. For the Democrats, the malapportionment question had two important dimensions: as an issue whose increasing popularity worked to their benefit; and, as a political reality, weakening what already may have been increased Democratic strength.

Iowa was quickly approaching a political impasse. The accelerated pace of social and economic change tore at the foundation of the state's political structure. Entrenched interest groups were visibly thwarting the popular will of Iowa's citizens. Those without knowledge of the state's history may have considered the plight irresolvable. But those more familiar with the state's progressive and third party traditions were not surprised to witness the rise of a "new" party, a party whose leaders demonstrated a desire to abolish the asylums of the reigning special interests and to reestablish a sense of majority rule. The "new" party was the revived Democratic Party of Iowa, jolted awake from its century-long dormancy.

Governor Herschel Loveless and Park Rinard, 1959
DES MOINES REGISTER

III

STIRRINGS IN POLK COUNTY: DEMOCRATS OF THE 1950s

THE DEMOCRATIC PARTY OF IOWA first reawakened during the early 1950s in the state's largest city, Des Moines. There a group of young and aggressive party workers attempted to tap the Democratic potential of an Iowa urban area. Concentrating initially on a few chosen precincts, these men and women learned political organization skills that they and others would later use in virtually every urban area in the state.

It was also in Des Moines that the new spirit of the modern party rose: an energetic approach to politics which anticipated and celebrated electoral victory, not defeat. This new spirit would prove contagious a few years later, when the Democratic leaders of Polk County (which included Des Moines), now in the capacity of state party leaders, delivered a creed of optimism and a strategy for victory to party members throughout Iowa, challenging for the first time their long-standing expectations of being vanquished.

The Republicans of Polk County, reigning continuously for decades, had grown reckless in the exercise of their power by the late 1940s. In 1946, for example, Republican members of the Polk County Board of Supervisors were jailed for illegal expenditures, leading to the election of a Democratic sheriff and Board member.[1] Harping on Republican political corruption, Wade P. Clarke, the newly-appointed Democratic county chairman, pointed to

A PARTY REBORN
— 38 —

other instances of such Republican "debauchery," hoping to garner backlash support for his own party's candidates in the 1948 election.

Throughout the 1940s, the Republicans used local patronage appointments to help bolster their party organization. Even grand jury appointments were handled on such a basis. Clarke attacked the GOP practice of using the judicial system to supply patronage slots for party workers. He claimed that the same people, all Republicans, were repeatedly appointed to grand jury duty, as if such duty were a steady job provided to party loyalists rather than a task assumed by citizens regardless of their political affiliations. Clarke then showed that several Republican appointees to the Polk County grand jury belonged to "key clubs" — clubs that served liquor-by-the-drink, skirting state law. In addition, Clarke and the Democrats scrutinized the methods by which absentee ballots were collected and counted. They suspected Republicans of inflating the GOP share of the approximately 13,000 absentee ballots turned into the auditor's courthouse office in the early 1940s. Clarke hired a private detective, told the press of his action, and positioned the detective in the auditor's office. There, on duty throughout each day, he counted the number of ballots turned in by registrars, reporting the totals to Clarke. As if to confirm Democratic suspicions, the 1948 absentee vote totals represented a serious decline for the county and for the GOP. Only about 5,000 such ballots were recorded that year. Partially in reaction to the visible Democratic efforts to expose Republican corruption, the public elected for the first time in history a majority of Democrats to the offices of the courthouse.

In an attempt to fix the image of corruption upon the surprised Republicans, on election day of 1948 Clarke and some of his Democratic colleagues denounced another mis-

STIRRINGS IN POLK COUNTY
— 39 —

use of power: Republicans had arranged to have mentally deficient people cast illegal and multiple ballots. Shortly before election day, they transferred to the Polk County Farm several Polk County residents who had been patients at the Clarinda State Mental Hospital in Page County. Then, as Chairman Clarke later explained, Republicans too enthusiastic for victory and too careless with power "loaded the insane people in autos to take them to precinct places in rural areas where no registration was required and they had them vote several times each... several of us [sent witnesses in] three cars [to the county farm] to watch the Republicans load the insane people in their cars and then followed them around and challenged them each time they voted. And we won each challenge."[2]

The charges of Clarke and his colleagues must have struck home. For with the 1948 election the Democrats of Polk County became the majority party in the courthouse. Once they were in power, Clarke took steps to ensure that the Democrats themselves did not fall into corruption through ill-conceived patronage appointments. At the same time, he deliberately rewarded enough of the party faithful with courthouse jobs to create a nucleus of workers for the upcoming campaigns:

With the '48 election success in the courthouse, we could have filled the place with patronage appointments, but we adopted a policy that those who were good in the past would be kept, in order to keep procedures in the courthouse running smoothly.... We were therefore able to create bipartisan support for the Democratic courthouse. Of course, I tried to find good jobs for the Democrats. We made an agreement: if men or women worked hard and were competent, they had a right to a courthouse job. If they deserved a job, but did not want one, they could select a replacement. Also, we made it policy that not more than one member per family could serve in the courthouse. These policies gave the Democrats incentive to work for and be loyal to the party. The Republicans had not created policies quite like this before.[3]

A PARTY REBORN

Unfortunately for the Democrats, courthouse patronage resembled federal patronage in that jobs awarded to party workers for past performance did not guarantee enthusiastic participation in future campaigns. The Polk County Democrats, however, demonstrated that they had learned from the mistakes of Chairman Jake More. A small group of younger party members stepped forward to assemble a party organization whose foundations were firmly embedded in the precincts of the county. They were determined not to let patronage appointments become the only source of party strength.

Neal Smith and Lex Hawkins, both lawyers, along with Robert L. Johnston, a leader from the United Auto Workers, dawned as the three most important party organizers in this period. Each man possessed qualities complementing the characteristics of the others, qualities that would prove assets in his later, separate career. Neal Smith, ambitious for high political office, would become the longest-serving Democratic member of Congress in Iowa history. Lex Hawkins, unequaled in tenacity and energy, would serve as state party chairman in the 1960s, and then practice as a successful attorney in Des Moines. And Robert L. Johnston, who brought with him the institutional support of the United Auto Workers and a knowledge of nuts-and-bolts politics learned directly from his friend Walter Reuther, would leave Iowa politics, after helping to initiate Polk County activism, to become an important operative in the national UAW.[4]

In 1952, Wade Clarke stepped down from his post as county chairman to give more attention to the law practice he shared with Neal Smith. Lex Hawkins succeeded him and immediately implemented a plan, devised by Robert Johnston and William Seymour, another labor activist, to canvass house-by-house the twelve Des Moines precincts

STIRRINGS IN POLK COUNTY

showing the most Democratic potential. The survey's purpose was to locate and identify Democratic voters. As one party worker, Michael Doyle, recalls:

> On a Saturday morning, Lex and I and some auto workers went out and went over to the east side to canvass to see if they were registered to vote and if they were Democrats. We found household after household of unregistered Democrats. Lex and I had walked all the way from University Avenue to Aurora and we were dusty and tired. He turned to me and said, "God, do you think we did any good?" It was sort of ironic, because that day was the start of the canvassing program, and it was extremely successful.[5]

Perhaps those canvassed did not realize Polk County Democrats were now recording their partisan inclinations, since the canvassers posed as public-opinion pollsters, interspersing bogus questions with the political ones. Party workers organized the names and addresses of those they identified as Democrats or Democratically-leaning independents into shoe box card files to be used in subsequent electioneering efforts.[6]

After precinct canvassers identified the thousands of potential Democrats, a problem arose: how to get these people registered to vote. At the turn of the century, when rural lawmakers had transformed the state's legislative apportionment from a population-based to an area-based system, they had also stipulated that persons residing in cities over 10,000 in population must be registered to vote, while those living in smaller communities or farms were not required to register. The law's impact was to amplify the problem of low voter participation in the urban areas. Republican-controlled courthouses in all "registration cities" opened only during those hours when laborers were at work, barring many potential voters—many of them Democrats—from the polls.

In a city the size of Des Moines, with about 220,000 people, the half-century-old law now imposed unrealistic restrictions. In addition to a six-month residency requirement, the law stipulated that all voters must register in person at the courthouse during regular office hours. Lex Hawkins's canvassing efforts had revealed a reserve army of potential Democratic voters who, for one reason or another, had not registered to vote. To remedy this situation, the Democrats and the League of Women Voters joined in 1952 to pressure City Council members to establish temporary registration sites at various locations across the city. In one three-day drive at 15 such sites, 8,500 persons registered to vote for the first time, many of them at the urging of Democratic Party workers. Based on the successful results in Des Moines, the League of Iowa Municipalities encouraged the state legislature to make neighborhood registration sites mandatory in all registration cities. But, predictably, the request fell on deaf ears; the rurally dominated, largely Republican General Assembly ignored the proposal.[7]

Fighting difficult odds on many fronts in the 1950s, the Polk County Democrats developed an unparalleled *esprit de corps*. When Wade Clarke had first assumed the county chairmanship in 1947, the monthly Central Committee meetings attracted only ten or twelve people. By the mid-1950s, however, with Lex Hawkins now serving as county chairman, the monthly meetings took place in the ballrooms of the Fort Des Moines and Savery hotels, with no less than 400 to 500 persons attending. Only about 200 of those present were voting members; the rest came for entertainment. Hawkins himself provided much of that entertainment. Able to create the heroic from the mundane, Hawkins elevated precinct leaders to the status of local stars. He brought the crowds to their feet to applaud party workers who had accomplished much on behalf of

STIRRINGS IN POLK COUNTY
— 43 —

the Democrats. Registration drives and election day efforts became Hawkins's stages on which he orchestrated the Polk County party drama.

In the earliest phase of Polk County organizational politics, Robert Johnston convinced the UAW to provide the several hundred dollars each year needed to finance registration and election day drives.[8] Within a few years, though, nearly $20,000 was necessary to cover the organizational expenses of the Polk County Democrats in an election year. Hundreds of Democrats now gathered in downtown Des Moines hotel ballrooms on the Sundays before election days. There, rousing the spirits of their workers with animated speeches, Lex Hawkins and his cohorts divided among the precinct captains the information accumulated from canvassing efforts. On voting day, these hundreds of Democrats filled the residential streets of many Des Moines precincts and pulled party members and sympathizers to the polls. Art Hedberg, who later served as Polk County chairman, recalled the routine prescribed for the first Tuesday of November: "On election day, we had maps drawn up for the precincts and we would work as teams. None had been paid for canvassing, but on election day we would often pay persons $15-$20 so that we would be sure to have enough people. We'd meet at 6:00 A.M. at headquarters and then at 7:00 A.M. we'd have the first of three rounds of door-knocking at the places we had identified."[9]

The Polk County Democrats produced positive results in stark contrast to the absence of results from Democrats in the rest of the state. Between 1946 and 1952, the percentage of eligible voters who went to the polls in Polk County exceeded the state average (see Figure 3). For example, between the off-year elections of 1946 and 1950, Polk County voter participation increased 11.5%, while other counties averaged an increase of just 8.2%. Polk County's in-

A PARTY REBORN
— 44 —

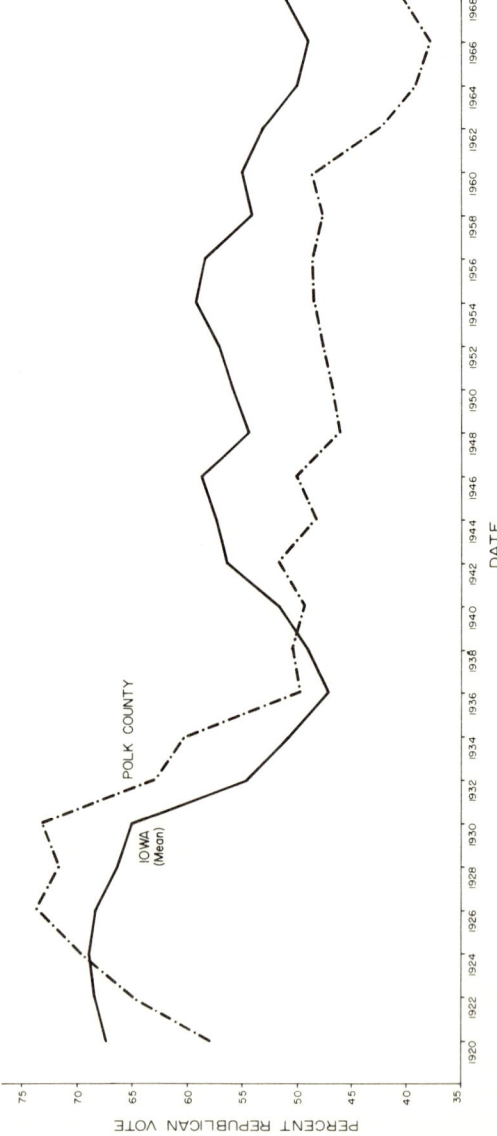

Figure 3. Partisan Preference of Iowa and Polk County Voters, 1920-1968

Source: George B. Mather, *Effects of the Use of Voting Machines on Total Votes Cast: Iowa—1920-1960* (Iowa City, Iowa, 1964), as updated by the author and James C. Larew.

STIRRINGS IN POLK COUNTY

crease between the presidential elections of 1948 and 1952 outdistanced the average state gain by a margin of 18.2% to 13.4%.[10]

In the election of 1954, the Democrats of Polk County achieved three "firsts." They won control of the county Board of Supervisors; they won every county administrative office; and most importantly, they won all Polk County state legislative seats.[11]

This series of victories stimulated the Des Moines Democratic leaders to renew attacks on State Chairman Jake More. Their confidence in the Democratic potential increased with their own successes, and made them even more impatient with More's less aggressive political style. In December of 1954, National Young Democrats president Neal Smith unleashed a blistering attack upon More in a letter to party leaders across the state: "I have had the opportunity to compare our state organization and campaigns with those of other states. The bare fact is that in comparison, our state organization is a mere 'holding organization'.... In the other states, there was a statewide organized effort [in the 1954 election] to support *all* candidates and especially the candidate for Senator, and there was also a plan for getting out the vote...." Claiming that the lack of a statewide organization comparable to Polk County's prevented Iowa Democrats from scoring more victories, Smith also charged More with failing to recruit new members to broaden the base of the party:

The fact is that Jake More [is] irrevocably identified with resisting...distribution of responsibility....Mr. More is also unfortunately identified with a perfect record of six successive defeats. There is not another state in the whole United States where the Democratic State Chairman has remained in office through six successive gubernatorial defeats.... It would be much easier to get new workers to rally behind

A PARTY REBORN

new leadership.... His [Jake More's] services under the circumstances, would be more valuable as an advisor.[12]

AS THE DEMOCRATS FOUND THEMSELVES on the verge of an internal revolt, the Republicans were increasingly torn by struggles of their own between progressive and conservative members. In the 1950s the progressive Republican leaders attempted to move their party to respond to the needs of labor and other urban groups, while conservative resistance in the legislature forestalled and frustrated almost every progressive effort. By the end of the decade, the leaders of the state's labor unions had transferred their loyalties to the Democratic Party, and such groups as the Iowa Farm Bureau Federation and the Iowa Manufacturers Association had reached the summit of their power among Republicans and rural Democrats.

In terms of total Republican victories in the 1950 elections, the GOP appeared to be as solid and powerful as ever. Recovering from the losses suffered two years earlier in the wake of Harry Truman's popularity, Iowa Republicans now regained 15 seats in the Iowa House (to total 94 of 108). They also retained the governorship and held onto a solid 43 to 7 margin in the Senate. All Republican Congressmen were re-elected by wider margins than in 1948. Veteran Republican U.S. Senator Bourke Hickenlooper won an easy victory in his race for a second term. Once again, the GOP had completely dominated the elections, as it had for 24 out of the past 25 off-year elections.[13]

But if the Republican state legislators agreed on party label, they nevertheless clashed on issues. The most deeply driven political wedge was the issue of labor laws. The growing bonds between organized labor and the Democrats of Polk County pointed to a possible new coalition between the two groups on a state-wide basis. Liberal Republicans wanted to stem the movement of labor out of

STIRRINGS IN POLK COUNTY

the GOP. At the 1950 state Republican convention, younger and more liberal members of the party forced themselves into positions of leadership. They prevailed upon the convention to endorse unanimously a plank calling for the repeal of the state's right-to-work laws. Echoing the demands voiced by labor unions for three years, the Republican platform now read:

> We hold that when any given labor organization has been chosen in a free and secret election by the employees of an individual industry to represent them in dealing with their employers, then all the employees of such industry should contribute to the cost of maintaining such organization or union. We are, therefore, not opposed to the union shop, provided the individual worker is protected against arbitrary expulsion from the union, and consequent loss of his job, by the mere whim or opinion of any union officer or officers or by pressure or intimidation from any fellow employee who may happen to disagree with him.[14]

In his inaugural message on January 11, 1951, moderate Republican Governor William Beardsley repeated that pledge to labor when he said: "I...recommend that the union shop be legalized. I further recommend that the individual workers be protected against arbitrary expulsion from the unions and consequent loss of jobs."[15] After the legislature convened, however, the dominant interest groups—bolstered by a disproportionately large number of rural and small-town legislators—prevented any decisive progressive moves. A last minute attempt to get a union-shop bill on the Iowa House calendar lost by a vote of 51 to 43, and the General Assembly adjourned, having failed to comply with the recommendations of the Republican platform and the party's own governor.[16]

In 1952, liberal Republicans again commanded enough power in the state convention to write progressive labor and farm planks. There was, in fact, very little difference between the platforms of the major parties that year. Both

A PARTY REBORN
— 48 —

came out strongly for the legalization of the union shop, and both advocated firm federal price support policies for farmers (Republicans called for full parity while Democrats supported a 90% price support level).[17] Riding the coattails of Dwight D. Eisenhower, the Republicans won the governor's chair and a record number of legislative races. They now held 105 of 108 House seats and 46 of 50 seats in the Senate. It was said that the Democrats held their caucuses in the Capitol phone booth.

But just as had happened two years earlier, the majority of the Republican legislators again refused to follow the recommendations of their own party's platform and governor. The year witnessed vicious political infighting. In February 1953, apparently as a result of internal divisions, the Republican state chairman made the unusual announcement that the state Central Committee would be unable to support or oppose any specific legislation before the upcoming General Assembly. As if further to underscore the difficulties of the GOP, state legislators simply avoided the controversial issues of the day. Instead, they chose to spend 100 days debating the question of legalizing the sale of colored oleomargarine.[18] That Governor Beardsley and his state party failed to direct legislative policy did not, of course, mean that the General Assembly was without directors. It meant, rather, that the interest groups—the IMA in particular—held considerably more power than the Republican Party itself.

Further intra-party rifts appeared as incumbent Attorney General Leo Hoegh sought the Republican nomination for governor. As Attorney General, Hoegh had created a stir when he insisted upon enforcing the state's liquor laws. A handsome man with a graying crew cut and mustache, Hoegh possessed unusual self-confidence. During World War II, he had directed the operations of the

STIRRINGS IN POLK COUNTY
— 49 —

17,000-member 104th Infantry ("Timberwolf") Division in its march to the Rhine River and into Germany. Combining his military approach to administrative detail with a surprisingly progressive political philosophy, he collided with those groups content to maintain the status quo.[19]

As a potential nominee for governor in 1954, Hoegh accurately perceived that the Republicans were about to lose the support of the state's largest labor organization, the State Federation of Labor, over the issue of labor laws. Republican Ray Mills, the Federation's president and also the mayor of Des Moines, had repeatedly expressed his disgust with the performances of successive Republican dominated General Assemblies.

Hoegh created an image of himself as an ally of labor by appointing a number of union members from across the state to a newly-formed Iowa Republican Labor Council. The Council's role, Hoegh indicated, would be to advise the party and the upcoming convention concerning desirable legislative initiatives. Mills, not a member of the Council, objected, claiming the Council's views were not those of the labor unions. Norman Miller, however, as chairman of the group, took positions remarkably similar to those Mills himself had earlier espoused. For example, the Council proposed that union shop agreements be legalized, that the remainder of the 1947 right-to-work laws be repealed, that the workmen's compensation and unemployment compensation laws be liberalized, and that the Labor Bureau of the state government be strengthened.[20] Finally, Council Chairman Miller admonished the Republican Party:

> Republicans in labor ranks have difficulty convincing other members of organized labor that the Republican Party intends in good faith to repeal the anti-union shop law.
> The 1952 Republican state convention endorsed repeal of the law ban-

A PARTY REBORN
— 50 —

ning the union shop but the 1953 legislature did not act. If you don't intend to carry out a platform pledge, we prefer that you don't put the pledge into the platform.

If the Republican Party will make an honest attempt to keep a platform pledge, it will win the support of 100,000 Iowa members of organized labor.[21]

At the 1954 state convention, Hoegh openly urged his party to support the positions taken by the Labor Council, while the IMA opposed them and threatened to withdraw its support of Hoegh if he remained adamant in his position. The IMA captured enough delegate strength to defeat the labor plank and, as if to dismiss completely the aspirations of labor, made certain that the platform ignored the Labor Council recommendations.[22]

Hoegh managed to win the Republican nomination despite his split with the IMA, but in the ensuing campaign he came under attack from all directions. Clyde E. Herring, his Democratic opponent, and son of former Governor Clyde L. Herring, attempted to take advantage of the conservative disenchantment with Hoegh and assumed a conservative-moderate posture. He accused Hoegh of supporting unnecessary tax increases and called him the handpicked successor of liberal Governor William Beardsley. At the same time, conservative Republicans withheld campaign contributions from Hoegh because of his pre-convention invitation to labor to share power in the party and because of his firm support of union shop contracts. Hoegh had taken both these pro-labor stands over the express objections of the IMA.[23]

Though battered by campaign fights, Hoegh nevertheless defeated his Democratic challenger because of the unwavering allegiances of small-town and farm voters to the Republican Party.[24] As the new governor, Hoegh perhaps represented the Iowa Republicans' final chance to keep all

STIRRINGS IN POLK COUNTY
— 51 —

major factions within the same party. He had openly opposed the state's conservative power brokers by supporting progressive causes, while managing to keep the backing of other conservative groups, like the Iowa Temperance Legislative Council, by calling for strict enforcement of the liquor-by-the-drink laws. But once in office, he found it even more difficult to battle the interest groups in the halls of the Iowa Capitol than on the floor of the state convention. Among the measures he proposed were: increased funding for education; a highway safety program; broadened promotion of industrial expansion; and legislative reapportionment. He struggled in vain to advance his progressive program over the objections of the representatives from rural and small-town areas who dominated the legislature. Hoegh was a hard-driving politician, and he publically expressed his disappointment when his own party did not act more decisively on his initiatives. In a futile attempt to pressure recalcitrant Republicans, the Governor sent out "scorecards" to members of the press and to Republicans across the state comparing the voting records of state legislators to the party platform and to Hoegh's own recommendations—a clear criticism of the legislature's performance.[25]

Hoegh's failure to counter the IMA effectively had precisely the result he feared; it drove union leadership into the Democratic camp. The Governor expressed his chagrin that the IMA had been able to thwart his efforts to liberalize the state's right-to-work statutes, but even his outward displays of disgruntlement could not soothe the anger and frustration of state AFL president Ray Mills. "All my life, I've been a registered Republican," Mills told the press in July of 1955. "I just got a little fed up with the promises of the Republican Party and its failure to go through with what it promised to labor people." He was, he announced,

A PARTY REBORN
— 52 —

switching his party affiliation to the Democrats.[26]

The Governor responded immediately, and somewhat desperately, by claiming Ray Mills's actions did not reflect the views of most Iowa workers. On behalf of Hoegh, Republican Party State Chairman Donald C. Pierson proclaimed the 1955 General Assembly had, indeed, made some improvements in the state's labor laws. Then, in an attempt to redefine the labor issue in urban-rural terms alone, Pierson chastised Mills's decision to join the Democrats, asking: "Do the labor leaders feel that an agricultural state such as Iowa should have the farmers in the legislature kicked out to serve the ends of the labor leaders?"[27]

The question implied that even moderates in the Republican Party did not fully comprehend the social transformations occurring in Iowa. Pierson's outburst provoked heated replies from labor leaders, replies that further widened the fissure between unions and the GOP. Edris "Soapy" Owens, a huge, determined man who had replaced Robert Johnston as head of the state CIO,[28] challenged Pierson to a public debate and ridiculed the Republican-dominated legislature, asserting that:

[The General Assembly] did not even attempt to meet the pitiful standards on those issues that had been recommended by President Eisenhower and the national Republican Party...I also am quite sure it does not meet the standards that Governor Hoegh feels are adequate. Do you wish to deny this publicly?

[State Chairman Pierson] has tried to drive a wedge between the farmer and organized labor by saying that we have added farmer legislators to the list to be attacked.[29]

And, as if to portend the future course of Iowa politics, Ray Mills, now a Democrat, warned pointedly: "The Iowa Manufacturers Association has been calling the shots too long."[30]

STIRRINGS IN POLK COUNTY
— 53 —

THOUGH EAGERLY EMBARKING ON A NEW ERA of political activism, labor rose to be an effective wielder of power through a slow and arduous process that required both the restructuring of internal union politics and the development of stronger ties among the unions. Ray Mills, for example, found his new preference for the Democratic Party opposed by many members of the federated unions. A. A. Couch, former head of Iowa's AFL, immediately challenged Mills for the presidency of the state organization and called Mills's change of political affiliation "childish." "Any federation president must deal with the Republican controlled Iowa legislature," Couch explained. "It certainly doesn't help labor in dealing with the legislature to have the federation president change his politics from Republican to Democratic."[31]

Mills survived the challenge strong enough to help lead the merger between his Federation and Iowa's CIO.[32] On June 27, 1956, Iowa became the twelfth state to witness a joining of AFL and CIO locals since the national merger two years earlier. The new Iowa Federation of Labor, AFL-CIO, at its first convention, elected Mills president. CIO head Soapy Owens, by this time also a member of the state Democratic Central Committee, was elected executive secretary in charge of political action.[33]

From this same convention, the new organization sent a clear message to the statehouse: the Democratic Party, not the Republicans, now had the support of labor. Herschel Loveless, the Democratic candidate for governor, addressed the more than 400 delegates in attendance, challenging them to become fully aligned with the Democratic Party. "You have this problem — you in labor," Loveless charged. "You have the record of people who are friendly to you, you have the problem of analyzing the political party that has been friendly to you. Once you have done that you have the responsibility as labor representatives of putting the finger on that particular party."³⁴ The AFL-CIO convention responded enthusiastically to Loveless and issued a platform similar to that of the Democratic Party in 1956. The union members called for repeal of the "misnamed right-to-work laws," an increase in unemployment and workmen's compensation allowances, repeal of the one-half cent sales tax imposed by the Hoegh administration, creation of a new minimum-wage law, and reapportionment of the Iowa legislature.³⁵

The new coalition of labor and the Democratic Party benefitted both bodies. Labor spent over $100,000 per election to support Democratic candidates. In return, the Democrats provided an agent through which labor groups could more easily pursue their legislative priorities, wants and needs. But the new alliance only partially explains the defeat of Governor Hoegh in 1956 and the election of Herschel Loveless as the fourth Democrat to serve in the governor's office since the Civil War. Easy victories in Iowa by Republicans Dwight D. Eisenhower for the presidency and Bourke Hickenlooper for the U.S. Senate demonstrated that the Loveless victory was exceptional.

Having risen from a job as parking meter salesman in Ottumwa, Herschel Loveless gained state-wide recognition in 1951 when, as mayor of that city, he guided emergency efforts to mitigate the hardships suffered when the Des Moines River flooded Ottumwa. Not highly educated, often speaking in roughcast sentences, Loveless was both energetic and aggressive, and Iowans responded favorably to him. One party worker of the time recalls:

> Herschel Loveless was unique. The norm for the Democrats at the time was to expect defeat, to cower in Democratic booths at county fairs and to speak only among fellow party members. The assumption was

STIRRINGS IN POLK COUNTY

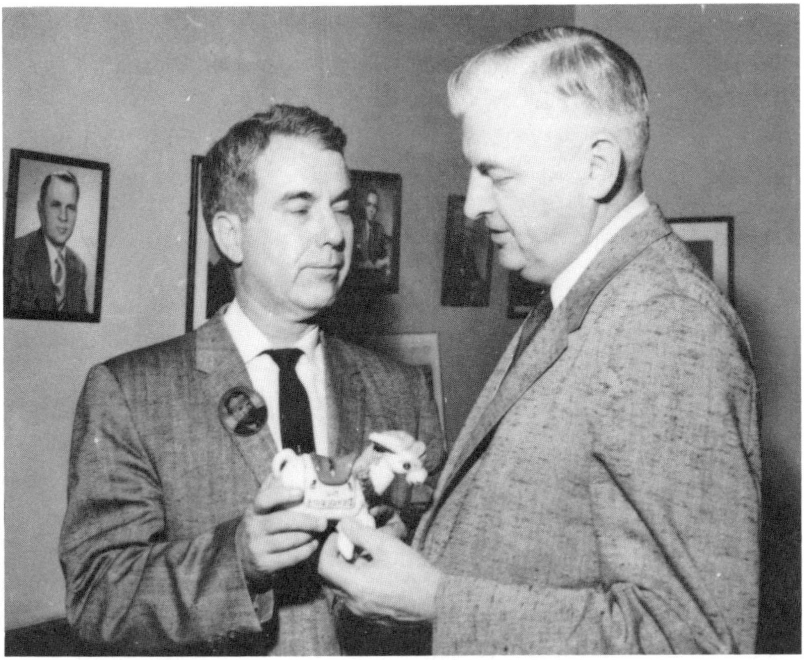

DES MOINES REGISTER

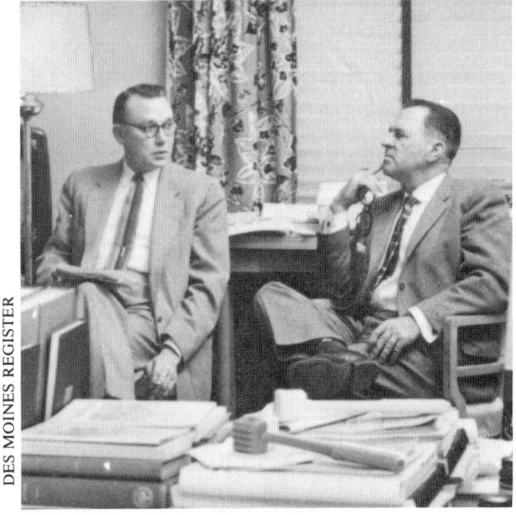

New Democratic Party Chairman Duke Norberg accepts a memento from fellow Democrat Jake More (above); Governor Herschel Loveless with Robert Johnson, 1958 (right)

DES MOINES REGISTER

always, "We'll never win, so why strain ourselves?" Loveless, though, was aggressive, and he pressed a lot of flesh. Loveless didn't hide in the fair booths, he courted the people.[36]

To go with his tireless style, Loveless employed a campaign strategy that successfully trapped Leo Hoegh in corners the Republicans themselves had created. In the course of his single term in office Hoegh had initiated capital gains and corporation taxes, and greater taxes on cigarettes, beer, and gasoline in order to finance his somewhat expanded social programs. Taxes are seldom popular, but one tax hike during the Hoegh years particularly unnerved Iowans — especially Governor Hoegh himself. Over his objections, the IMA had gathered forces sufficient to override a possible veto and forced the Governor into signing a bill raising the state sales tax from 2 to 2.5%. Loveless made good use of the issue and stung Governor Hoegh with a campaign epithet: "High Tax Hoegh." Meanwhile, the IMA, having already hurt the Governor by increasing the sales tax, punished him further by withdrawing its support because of his refusal to champion right-to-work laws.

At the same time, after several years of surplus production and depressed market prices, Iowa farmers renewed their volatile political habits. The Eisenhower Administration, through Ezra Taft Benson's outspoken guidance as Secretary of Agriculture, had proposed dealing with the problem through a program of flexible price supports that could be lifted as market prices began to rise. The national Democratic Party responded by proposing high and permanent price support levels, as well as production controls and direct payments to farmers when needed.[37]

The Iowa Farm Bureau Federation continued to back the Republican Administration, but many Iowa farmers strongly resisted the Benson policies. Iowa Democratic Na-

STIRRINGS IN POLK COUNTY

tional Committeeman Donald J. Mitchell wrote a briefing paper for Democratic presidential candidate Adlai E. Stevenson that outlined farm sentiment:

> At this time, of course, the dominant issue in this State is the farm price situation. There is no doubt in my mind that unless drastic remedies and corrective measures are taken that this State will support all Democratic Candidates in the Fall election. We are having rallies and meetings throughout the State most of which I attend. We are going into counties where in 1952 we had very little support and now these meetings are attended by hundreds of people. Friends of mine who are dealing with the farmers continually state that the farmers have definitely turned from the Republican Party and will be with us in the Fall.[38]

The serious predicament of the farmers and the volatile nature of their political behavior ultimately left Hoegh without strong farm allies. On several occasions Hoegh attempted to advise Secretary Benson, only to be rebuffed. The Governor responded by denouncing Benson as "inflexible." As a result, although Hoegh endorsed the Republican concept of flexible price supports, the IFBF, backing both Benson and Benson's policies, took offense at the Governor's outspoken manner. Like the IMA, it withdrew active support from him.[39] The rest of the Iowa farmers, many of whom agreed with neither the Governor nor Secretary Benson on price support policies, gravitated toward Herschel Loveless when he unequivocally embraced the national Democratic platform.

The last important issue in 1956 was liquor-by-the-drink. Leo Hoegh had made his most visible mark in Iowa politics, first as attorney general and then as governor, advocating strict enforcement of the liquor laws. But by now a clear majority of Iowans, primarily those living in the urban areas, favored changing those laws. Loveless shared that desire for change. In expressing his views, he helped cement the political allegiances of Iowa's urban voters to his own candidacy.[40]

A PARTY REBORN

By focusing his attacks upon high taxes, low farm prices, and unpopular liquor laws, Loveless kept Hoegh on the defensive throughout the campaign. Even though the two men agreed on most other essential issues (both opposed extension of the last half-cent sales tax adopted by Hoegh's legislature, while favoring development of a progressive tax structure, more equitable reapportionment, legalization of the union shop contracts, and expanded industrialization of the state), Hoegh, ironically, had created a more liberal image for himself than his opponent—an image sufficiently liberal to alienate many conservative Iowa voters.[41] As Hoegh lost the support of labor, Herschel Loveless attracted a substantial portion of the conservative vote even though he was the candidate of the party that had struggled for over a decade to establish itself as the progressive political force in the state. Loveless, in winning a larger percentage of the vote than all but two gubernatorial candidates since 1885, observed: "Leo Hoegh helped elect me in many ways. He was liberal when he thought that was popular, then he would shift to the conservative side when he sensed that was more popular. The nominal Republicans didn't want a liberal—they wanted me because they perceived me as being more conservative than Hoegh. A moderate/conservative split was occurring in the state."[42]

Once in office, Loveless faced serious obstacles from the start. First, by constitutional design, the governorship of Iowa was a weak office. Virtually all administrative powers ordinarily assigned to a chief executive were limited by state statutes. Second, even though he had carried more Democrats into the legislature than had served at one time since 1937 (there were now 36 House and 10 Senate Democrats), his party still lacked the one-third membership required to block Republican threats of overriding his

STIRRINGS IN POLK COUNTY

vetoes. Finally, conservative Republicans chaired the most important committees and controlled the flow of legislation to the floor of the General Assembly.[43]

In his first term, from 1957 to 1959, Loveless did fulfill his campaign pledge to veto extension of the one-half cent sales tax hike imposed by the previous administration. But the Governor's most important contributions to Iowa politics were not legislative. He was widely praised for the unusually high caliber of his appointments to state commissions and boards. When he realized the rural members of the legislature were ill-disposed to reapportioning themselves, he appointed two well-publicized committees to deliberate the reapportionment question. The Governor's Reapportionment Action Committee, headed by associate editor Frank Nye of the *Cedar Rapids Gazette,* and composed of 15 additional state leaders, met over a four-year period to create a proposal for a just reapportionment plan. A second group, the Commission on Economic and Social Trends in Iowa, known also as the "Committee of One Hundred," recommended a thorough change in state legislative representation.[44]

Loveless's most spectacular, if not perhaps his most important, contribution to the Democratic Party during his first term was the deft and sudden ouster of Jake More from the state chair in the summer of 1958. Two years earlier, in 1956, with the support of Neal Smith and Wade Clarke, Lex Hawkins had defeated Clyde E. Herring, Jake More's closest ally, to become a member of the State Central Committee. At his first meeting, Hawkins had made an unusual request; he had asked that the press be allowed to attend the Committee's session. He then proceeded to call for a vote to oust Jake More. Not surprisingly, Hawkins had lost the vote by a margin of 15-1, but his diatribes against More received front-page, state-wide publicity.[45]

A PARTY REBORN

In the two years following his first attempt, Hawkins had worked to recruit candidates for the State Central Committee who would vote to oust More. He had rallied support for these candidates from Democrats across the state in anticipation of the 1958 state convention, which was to elect members to the Committee.[46] At the convention, events moved so rapidly that even some of the principal characters involved were uncertain of the origin and the meaning of the anti-More upsurge. The Governor's consent was essential to the overthrow. Loveless made it clear to his closest aide, Bob Johnson, that he wanted More removed, in accordance with the openly expressed wishes of Lex Hawkins, Soapy Owens, and others. These men wanted Hawkins himself to be chairman. Loveless remembered: "I didn't actively move Jake out, but let's put it this way, I could have prevented it if I had wanted to. Lex Hawkins was one of a dozen county chairmen and the like who were quite active in dumping Jake. I put Duke Norberg in the state chair to succeed Jake. I didn't want to put the seat up for grabs. Duke Norberg was an old friend from Albia."[47] To choose Duke Norberg, an unknown, personable, small-town newspaper reporter, as state chairman was an astute political compromise. Though Lex Hawkins desired the seat, many rural, conservative members of the party disliked him because of their strong loyalties to Jake More. Norberg's brief service as chairman would provide a needed buffer between the radically different approaches to politics More and Hawkins embodied.

If Loveless and Johnson had decided in advance that they would replace More with Norberg, they kept the decision secret even from Norberg himself, who was undoubtedly the most surprised person at the convention. Reflecting upon the turn of events, Norberg recalled his

STIRRINGS IN POLK COUNTY
— 61 —

own astonishment when he found himself heir to the More legacy and on the forefront of Democratic politics: "I had no idea that I would be the state chairman. Frankly, I was pessimistic.... I thought the movement [to oust More] was not well organized and felt it was certain to meet the fate that similar movements had had before. Some people interested in changing state chairmen had suggested that I run for the office, but I hadn't given it a thought."[48] No doubt Johnson had prompted the words of encouragement which Norberg mentioned. His scheming worked perfectly. On the opening day of the convention, when no other candidates had announced to run against Jake More, Norberg "volunteered" himself for the post. As Norberg remembered the event, he approached others in anticipation of defeat saying: "Hell, we can't win now. I have no ambitions. I'll run."[49]

But Norberg did win. A 12-4 vote of the Central Committee ended a tenure longer than those of six contemporary Republican state chairmen put together. Enraged, More drove to the party headquarters in the Hotel Fort Des Moines and proceeded to destroy many state party records, as well as letters to delegates, contributor lists, pencils and scratch paper. When Duke Norberg arrived for work at the office the next day, the place had been gutted. More had finally been unseated from the state chairmanship, but Democratic leaders would continue to feel his presence for several years to come.[50]

IN HIS 1958 CAMPAIGN for a second term as governor, Loveless was opposed by William Murray, a moderate Republican and professor of economics at Iowa State University in Ames. In virtually every area except labor laws and taxes, both the Republican Party and Murray himself were determined to present a liberal message to Iowa voters. The race was extremely close, and it divided the major interest groups in the state. The IMA and the Iowa State Education Association backed Murray, while for the first time ever, all member unions of the now merged AFL-CIO endorsed Loveless and the entire Democratic ticket. Initially the campaign focused on taxation. Murray contended that extra funds were needed to finance expanded social programs—especially schools—and that a sales tax increase of 1% would have to be imposed. Loveless, just as he had done two years earlier against Hoegh, charged that increased sales taxes were unnecessary and regressive. Early in the campaign, the issue appeared to give neither candidate a decisive advantage.[51]

Suddenly, however, Loveless gained the upper hand when Murray attempted to tie the Governor to the alleged illegal activities of the Teamsters Union and its president, Jimmy Hoffa. Actually, the Governor was well prepared for the change thanks to a tip coincidentally given him by Duke Norberg before the 1958 convention. Norberg explained: "In '58, I was working for a newspaper down in Albia. A friend of mine from Washington, D.C.—a source I trusted—called me to tell me that Bill Murray, Herschel Loveless's next opponent, was going to 'zero-in' on the relationship that had developed between the state party organization—that meant Jake More—and the Teamsters Union. I called Loveless and told him this."[52]

Murray's campaign release implied that Loveless had paid off his previous campaign debts to then-Party Chairman Jake More from a sizable contribution made to him by Teamsters President Hoffa. Loveless quickly turned the poorly substantiated charge to his own advantage, demanding a full explanation and an apology from Murray. When neither explanation nor apology came forth, the Governor refused to shake his opponent's hand at a well-

STIRRINGS IN POLK COUNTY

publicized joint appearance. Public sympathy flowed to the accused Loveless.[53]

The Teamsters controversy gave Loveless campaign momentum, but in the end, according to Iowans polled after the election, the sales tax issue proved to be the most important factor in Loveless's 1958 victory.[54] He carried 63 of 99 counties, including the urban areas and much of the cash-grain farm sector. With him, 50 Democratic House members and 12 Democratic senators won election to the legislature. A stunning four of eight Democrats were elected to Congress, one of them Neal Smith in the Fifth Congressional District, which encompassed Polk County, where the Democrats won 54.6% of the vote. The citizens of Iowa had clearly registered their dissatisfaction with the Eisenhower agricultural policies and their approval of Herschel Loveless's first term as governor. Still, the GOP, having retained substantial majorities in the state House and Senate, as well as complete control of three-fourths of the county courthouses in the state, clearly dominated Iowa politics.[55]

Although the primary issue of the campaign had been taxes, the major concern of the 58th General Assembly became reapportionment.[56] Several important factors caused the question to be brought before the legislature. First, Loveless now had enough potential support to blunt threats made by the Republicans to override his veto. Virtually all of this increased strength derived from the state's urban areas. Second, a ground swell of support for reapportionment had risen in the state conventions of both political parties. In their platforms of 1958, both had strongly endorsed some form of legislative redistricting. Even the conservative interest groups, it seemed, now agreed that some form of reapportionment would be necessary.

Because of the ambiguity of the consensus for reapportionment, however, opinion within the legislature diverged widely as to how the boundaries should be redrawn. The practical effect of state constitutional amendments in 1904 and 1928 had been to transform the apportionment of the Senate from a population-based to an area-based system. The rural areas, as their population continued to diminish, retained an increasingly disproportionate share of legislative seats. On the one hand, the rurally-oriented interest groups and members preferred plans of reapportionment that would retain as much of the land bias as possible. On the other hand, the most progressive members of the legislature wished to reapportion both houses according to population. They realized, though, that such a plan would never be approved by the present General Assembly. The debate in the legislature, then, centered on the question of what compromise between area-based and population-based apportionment might be struck.

In the 1955 legislative session, five urban Republican state senators had asked the Iowa Legislative Research Bureau to analyze the reapportionment question and to compare Iowa's experience with that of other states. The analysis, published in 1956, had recommended that the legislature reapportion itself along "federal" lines—that is, one house according to population and the other by area. From that point on, legislators debated which of the chambers, the House or the Senate, should be districted according to population and which according to land area.[57]

In 1958, there were 50 members of the Senate and 108 members of the House. Rural members of both chambers, eager to retain as much area bias as possible, supported those plans calling for the larger House to be apportioned according to area (preferably, one representative per county). The Senate, being smaller in size though apportioned

STIRRINGS IN POLK COUNTY

according to population, would necessarily be composed of members representing larger land areas, an arrangement again tending to favor the rural residents. Urban members argued that such plans implied "upside-down and backwards" thinking about the federal model. They insisted that the larger House, where each member represented fewer constituents than did each member of the Senate, should be apportioned according to population, so its members could more truly represent popular will. According to their logic, the smaller Senate would be the preferable chamber for area-based districting.

In essence, the reapportionment controversy represented a rural-urban conflict. As the most hotly contested issue to face Iowa legislators in many years, it tended to divide political parties and interest groups along predictable lines. The Republican Party, reflecting the strains of the rural-urban conflict within its own ranks, had recommended in its 1958 platform the passage of a reapportionment plan calling for either the House or the Senate to be redistricted according to population. The Democrats, in contrast, articulated primarily urban sentiments. They maintained that the House, specifically, should be the population-based chamber.

Once the session began, there developed two insurmountable obstacles to substantial reform. First, members of each chamber expressed their willingness to redraw the districts of the other chamber. Fearful of losing their own seats, however, they refused to have themselves reapportioned. Second, and more significantly, the power of interest groups outweighed the power of either political party. This was the particular session when every House committee was chaired by an IFBF member. Robert Fulton, a liberal Democrat from Waterloo, later to become lieutenant governor and, briefly, governor, served his first term in the Senate starting in 1959. He explained the magnitude of this second obstacle: "The reapportionment battle was one between the urban interests and the Farm Bureau. We'd pass a particular bill in the House, and then it would get killed in the Senate. We'd caucus in the day, and the Farm Bureau would caucus at night in a downtown hotel with all its members. That's where the power was, and the members were not able or willing to buck the Farm Bureau pressures."[58]

In fact, members of the IFBF had quietly written their own proposal for reapportionment, and they now loudly supported it, calling it the Shaff Plan—after Senator David O. Shaff of Clinton—to disguise their authorship.[59] First written during the 1955 session of the legislature, the Shaff Plan called for a Senate based on population and a House based on area. Shaff would later describe the motivation behind his reapportionment efforts: "Labor sees within their grasp the possibility of getting a complete transfer of power from rural Iowa, the lesser populated areas, to urban centers of high population so that the larger counties could control the Legislature."[60]

Indeed, labor vigorously supported reapportionment which treated the urban areas more equitably, but the AFL-CIO was hardly alone. Joining with it to work for a new redistricting scheme were such groups as the League of Women Voters, virtually all the urban press (led by the *Cedar Rapids Gazette* and the *Des Moines Register*), Democratic party leaders, and even some urban Republicans.

It became apparent that the legislators' reluctance to lose their own seats and the Farm Bureau's power could combine to prevent effective redrawing of legislative district lines. Fighting back, Democrats in the legislature (and later in the state Democratic platform meeting as well) promoted a constitutional convention referendum in the 1960 election. The will of the people, they reasoned, could thwart the domination of special interests. Urban groups joined to sponsor the convention, forming an organization called the Non-Partisan Citizens Committee for a Constitutional Convention. But they were completely overwhelmed in the campaign by the organizational abilities and the financial resources of rural and small-town organizations. The expenditures of the IMA and the IFBF alone totaled nearly two million dollars in 1959, while the expenditures of the Iowa League of Women Voters and the AFL-CIO together totaled only about $100,000.[61]

In their campaign against the convention, the IMA and IFBF called for reapportionment of the legislature, but according to the dictates of the legislature itself, not by means of a constitutional convention. They portrayed a convention as a potential power orgy where organized labor would completely restructure the Iowa political system to its own advantage. In response, the urban press and the Democrats pointed out that on such key issues as taxation, liquor-by-the-drink, and labor laws,[62] a minority of the population continued, via their state legislators, to sabotage the will of the majority. The General Assembly, they said, had repeatedly refused to enact a fair plan for reapportionment. On the contrary, the progressive coalition maintained, a constitutional convention presented the only reasonable way to reinstate majority rule in Iowa.

Republicans split on the 1960 ballot question. Rural forces won 53 to 47%, by consolidating both Republican and Democratic votes. In all other campaigns in 1960, however, urban and rural Republicans alike joined to score victories over the Democrats. The campaign for governor was marked by unusually emotional debates over the issues. Lieutenant Governor Edward M. McManus, the

A PARTY REBORN
— 68 —

Democratic candidate and close friend of Jake More, had defeated Commerce Commissioner Harold E. Hughes for the nomination. Now McManus attempted to make the constitutional convention an issue in his campaign. Following the Democratic platform, he called for the adoption of a plan by the convention to apportion Senate seats according to area and House seats in proportion to population distribution. Attorney General Norman Erbe, his Republican opponent, adhered to the vague position of his own party. At the Republican state convention, the IFBF and the IMA had opposed the constitutional convention, but initially agreed to support a plank stipulating that some form of a "federal plan" should be adopted. They then waited until the late, weary hours of the convention to knock that same plank out of the platform. As a result, the platform actually adopted by the Republicans only hinted at support for legislative reapportionment and offered no specific guidelines for creating a more equitable plan. Nor did the Republicans, in the end, endorse or reject the idea of a constitutional convention. Following his party's suit, Erbe said during his campaign both that he would probably vote for the convention on election day and that such a convention was unnecessary and undesirable.[63]

The race for United States Senator was tight. Before the campaign, incumbent Republican Thomas Martin declined to seek a second term in a surprise announcement following publicized charges of nepotism against him. With Martin now out, it looked as though Governor Loveless would glide to an easy victory over challenger Jack Miller, who had barely been able to win the Republican nomination.[64] In 1960, however, Loveless did not have the issues he had had in 1956 (Hoegh's tax increase) or in 1958 (William Murray's vitriolic campaign tactics) to usher him into office. As late as September 1960 less than one out of six

STIRRINGS IN POLK COUNTY
— 69 —

Iowans could identify Jack Miller, according to a private poll conducted by Louis Harris. Even so, the poll indicated that 45% of the voters favored the so-called "faceless wonder" Republican. Party loyalty, it appeared, still determined how Iowans voted. So that he might not help Miller become better known, the pollster advised Loveless "to campaign and campaign hard on issues and on his [the Governor's] record and personality—and flatly ignore his opponent... the campaign strategy... does not include any provisions for meeting or even discussing Miller."[65] Because Loveless followed the latter part of this recommendation, Miller was able to stump the state, staging televised "empty chair debates" against an opponent who refused to make joint appearances. Loveless's aloofness began to seem a serious mistake.

Some observers also believed that Loveless had taken in unseemly fashion the vice-presidential bait dangled before him by John F. Kennedy. Loveless ignored Miller, but unfortunately ignored his own campaign as well. Flying to all corners of the country, he made speeches concerning farm policy on Kennedy's behalf. In the meantime, Jack Miller was becoming better known to Iowans as he completed a 62,000-mile, 14-month campaign. In the end, Loveless's campaigning for the vice-presidency had two results. Most importantly, it took him out of the state when his own campaign needed attention. Second, it associated him with the liberal Catholic Senator Kennedy, an unlikely favorite in predominantly Protestant Iowa, a state where many of the Catholics hold conservative views. The 171,816-vote margin by which Richard M. Nixon defeated Kennedy in Iowa helped boost Miller's margin over Loveless to 47,344 votes.[66]

Behind the strong lead of Richard Nixon and the surprising success of Jack Miller, the GOP enjoyed an abundance of victories, reminiscent of earlier decades when the party easily dominated Iowa politics. The Republicans captured all but two congressional seats, sending six legislators to join Miller in Washington. At the statehouse, the GOP gained an overwhelming advantage, holding on to all statewide offices (such as lieutenant governor, secretaries of state and agriculture, and state treasurer) while capturing commanding majorities in both chambers of the General Assembly—they now held a 78-30 margin in the House and a 35-15 lead in the Senate.

But such victories shortly precipitated renewed Republican difficulties. As a larger and now more distinct majority, the GOP became responsible for the same issues that had haunted the party throughout the 1950s. Although the constitutional convention proposal had been defeated, many more Iowans now took greater interest not only in reapportionment but in liquor-by-the-drink and the modification of labor laws as well. The new Republican governor, unable to transcend the divisions within his own party, proved to be extraordinarily indecisive on all these major issues, and the 59th General Assembly showed itself incapable of writing significant progressive legislation.

As for the Democrats, it may have appeared to some that the overwhelming defeats of the 1960 campaign had devastated the hopes of those who sought to revive that party. Loveless, a symbol of many of those hopes, departed for Washington to accept a Kennedy appointment to the Federal Renegotiation Board. Party Chairman Norberg, who had typified the party's structural metamorphosis from the Jake More years, resigned his post to become a speech writer for Kennedy's secretary of agriculture, Orville Freeman.

Despite appearances, Democratic and progressive hopes, if diminished, had not been extinguished. Into the

STIRRINGS IN POLK COUNTY

vacuum of leadership strode the strongest leaders in the party's history. Lex Hawkins, appropriately describing himself as a "dictator," followed the script he had helped to write at the 1958 convention to become the new Democratic state chairman. From that position, he would force the urban areas of the state to learn the hard lessons of the organizational politics he himself had learned in Polk County.

To complement the party's new organizational efforts, a new leader would arise to capture the imagination not only of his own party, but of the entire state. Harold E. Hughes, as a person and as a symbol, more than anyone or anything else, would provide Democrats with a renewed sense of their progressive political mission. It was he who would convince members of the Democratic Party to expect victory, not defeat, at the polls.

Governor Harold Hughes in the State House, 1964
GEORGE TAMES/NEW YORK TIMES PICTURES

IV

THE DEMOCRATS REBORN: THE RISE OF HAROLD HUGHES

IN THE 1960S AMERICA WITNESSED the national emergence of an issue-oriented public, one less bound by the partisan loyalties of the past.[1] Joined to this national public through the media of mass communication, Iowans engaged in impassioned debate over such crucial social issues as domestic race relations and America's involvement in the Vietnam War. Jarred by the divisive force of these issues, Iowans shared the new independent instincts of the rest of the nation and increasingly abandoned the partisan political allegiances that, only a decade earlier, had provided an important source of political stability. By 1976, fully one-third of Iowa voters would deny allegiance to any political party.

Given the general relationship between national political trends and Iowa's own, it is ironic that it was in the 1960s that the Democratic Party of Iowa rose from its century-long quiescence to become one of the more vibrant state party organizations in the country. This growth occurred in two distinct yet overlapping phases. A singular political figure—Harold E. Hughes—dominated the initial phase, lasting roughly from 1962 to 1970. Answering the impatient desires of Iowans for effective leadership, Hughes offered a bold political style addressing directly the important issues of the day. He ushered the state from an era of rural control to a period of urban-rural cooperation. He acted as a catalyst, crystalizing a new image for his party.

A PARTY REBORN
— 74 —

Under Hughes, Iowa Democrats increasingly focused their attention on the social concerns engaging the nation. With Hughes as governor, Lex Hawkins, the audacious Democratic party chairman, careered through the state attempting to stimulate organizing efforts in other urban areas modeled after his own remarkably successful Polk County system. Despite his sustained efforts, Hawkins could not sufficiently establish organizations strong enough to survive his resignation as state chairman in 1966. And Hughes himself, an immensely charismatic politician in an unusual era, never showed much concern for the details of nuts-and-bolts political organization.

Therefore, it would take a second phase of activity — one of increasing and unprecedented statewide organization — for the Democratic Party to consolidate its initial gains. In the 1970s the impetus for organizational politics flowed not from Polk County leaders but largely from energetic Congressman John C. Culver of eastern Iowa's Second District and his equally vigorous colleague, Richard C. Clark. These two men, in several years of surging political success in the Second District, synthesized Culver's aggressive, issue-centered approach to politics with Clark's time-tested and computerized methods of precinct-by-precinct organization. When Culver and Clark used these techniques in statewide contests in the 1970s, both were elected to the United States Senate. With their modern campaign methods, the Democratic Party, for the first time since before the Civil War, became the dominant political party in a newly competitive two-party state.

THE UNRESOLVED REPUBLICAN DILEMMA of the 1950s haunted Republican Governor Norman Erbe's only term of office. The same rural, conservative forces that eclipsed the political career of Leo Hoegh in 1956 still commanded

DEMOCRATS REBORN

political control. The outright clashes between Hoegh, the Iowa Manufacturers Association, and the Iowa Farm Bureau Federation had provided widely visible displays of the underlying conflicts within the GOP. But during Erbe's short tenure progressive Republicans were more subdued as interest groups vied for power quietly in the legislative cloakrooms.

Responding to demands of insurgents in both parties, the 59th General Assembly (1960-61) did pass some significant legislation. However, legislators failed to contend with taxes and reapportionment, the two most important issues of the day. Completely ignoring the problem of rising taxes, the General Assembly declined to readjust the tax structure and ease the financial burdens caused by schools, local governments, and increased state-supported social services.

As for reapportionment, the rural legislators gained enough support from urban Republican moderates to pass the IFBF-penned Shaff Plan. Because the plan still continued to favor rural and small-town areas, the urban press and Democrats in the legislature quickly moved to the attack, calling the new system the "Shaft Plan." Eager to label it a Republican creation, State Chairman Hawkins directed all Democrats in the Senate to oppose it. Democratic Senator Adolph Elvers, from the small town of Elkader, defied Hawkins and became the only one of 15 party members to support the plan. With Elvers's backing, the Senate approved the plan and Hawkins retaliated in unprecedented fashion. Hawkins demanded Elvers, who had twice pledged his opposition to the plan, be barred from future Democratic caucuses. Democratic legislators denied the request.[2]

The General Assembly failed to confront convincingly the state's most important needs, in part, because Governor Erbe failed to provide assertive and independent leadership. Erbe claimed the political vision of the era was obscured "by a torrential rain of empty slogans, false charges, and meaningless phrases." Using his own situation as an example, the governor continued:

> The verbal storm caused by the thunder on the right and the lightning on the left has beclouded his [the voter's] sight. Radical conservatism looks into a past for a golden age that never existed. Radical liberalism looks into the future for a golden age that never will exist. Conservatism seeks to cultivate the "homely" virtues supposedly possessed by the independent yeomen of the Old Frontier. Liberalism seeks to cultivate the "sophisticated" virtues supposedly possessed by the clever gentlemen of the New Frontier.
> One extreme would regress to the economic license of "laissez-faire." The other extreme would progress to the economic tinkering of a "managed economy." It is the solemn duty of Republicans to fill this gaping ideological and pragmatic void.³

Erbe's own explanations for the legislative deadlock between conservative and liberal forces are rather remarkable. "Solemn" he may have been, but Erbe was unable to fill the void of leadership in the state. In direct contrast to the man who would campaign against him in 1962, Governor Erbe's explanation of his refusal to intervene in legislative battles is also noteworthy:

> Only the General Assembly has the constitutional right to make laws. The governor can sign a bill, let it become law without his signature, or veto it.... No matter which political party controls the governor's office, responsible administration of our state government demands the firm recognition of the fact that the lawmaking rights of our state are only within the domain of the legislature. If we ever have a governor who ignores the doctrines of our constitution because of a greedy and destructive philosophy, we shall then see the beginning of decay of free government we now possess and, in its place, the seed of the malignant shape of dictatorship and totalitarianism.⁴

If an assertive governor was akin to dictatorship, then apparently Iowans desired a benevolent dictator because

DEMOCRATS REBORN

Erbe's challenger in 1962, Harold E. Hughes, gained rapid public support when he labelled his opponent "No Stand Norman."[5] Hughes launched a billboard campaign that read "New Strength for Iowa," and he journeyed across the state presenting clearly defined stands on all salient issues. His call for legalization of liquor-by-the-drink received special attention.

An admitted and abstaining alcoholic, Hughes argued the existing liquor statutes, because they lacked public support, were impossible to enforce and created an atmosphere of hypocrisy in the state. The *Des Moines Sunday Register,* for example, had discovered that business establishments in at least two-thirds of Iowa's counties harbored illegal bars.[6]

When Erbe refused to take a stand on the liquor question, he further underscored the central theme of his challenger's campaign. Hughes claimed that the incumbent governor did not supply Iowa with the leadership it needed. Backed strongly by Iowa's urban areas, Hughes won a comfortable margin in an election with few other Democratic victories.[7]

WHEN HAROLD E. HUGHES EMERGED as the solitary standard-bearer of the Democratic Party in January of 1963, he had laid the groundwork for one of the most amazing political careers in the state's history. Hughes's political pilgrimage would lead him eventually to the United States Senate and to an aborted try for the presidency in 1972, followed shortly thereafter by his surprising decision to leave the Senate to devote his life to Christian lay work. Upon the announcement of his retirement from the Senate in 1973, the *Des Moines Register* wrote, "Harold Hughes had not completed his second term as governor of Iowa when it became obvious that state government would never

A PARTY REBORN

be the same again. Or state politics."⁸ Indeed, the Democratic Party of Iowa to a significant degree became the personal party of Harold Hughes, and under his leadership it gained power, prestige, and to a large extent, a new constituency.

Hughes's dramatic success resulted from three related factors: his outspoken, issue-oriented, and adventurous approach to politics (at an especially appropriate historical moment); his keen political advisors (who augmented his own ability to translate progressive and sometimes alien ideas into the "common sense" sentiments of the state's citizens); and a personal charisma which forged a renewed sense of community among Iowans who had been fragmented by the rapid changes of the postwar years.

The style of Harold Hughes, one of "forthrightness and candor that are exceptional in politics,"⁹ was astonishing in its contrast to that of earlier Iowa politicians. It was also a style peculiarly well adapted to the new political realities of the 1960s, both in Iowa and throughout the nation.

During the Eisenhower years and before, many American voters had defined themselves by their unwavering party affiliations, often inherited from ethnic and family traditions. For the most part, only uncommonly strong personalities or unusually successful or inept administrations caused temporary changes in the allegiances of voters; less often had partisan loyalties been based upon the policy alternatives of opposing parties or candidates.¹⁰

By the early 1960s, however, American political behavior had altered dramatically. A candidate's personality remained important, but a new cluster of political issues now also played a critical role in final voter choices. Party loyalties became much less important in determining voting patterns. The change from the Eisenhower to the Kennedy/Johnson Administration, and the subsequent Goldwater-Johnson presidential race of 1964, served to clarify previously muddled issue orientations of the voters. That new era also more clearly delineated differences between conservative and liberal positions on major social questions. The emerging social issues, those concerning race relations, war, welfare, income distribution, and size of government, were no longer seen as abstract matters, but as important problems impinging directly upon the lives of most individual citizens.[11] A new concern for these issues now infused American politics. Voters became much more sophisticated, much more concerned with political issues than they had been only a decade earlier. Observing this trend, Professor Sidney Verba and his colleagues concluded: "The American public has been entering the electoral arena since 1964 with quite a different mental set than was the case in the late 1950s and early 1960s. They have become more concerned with issues and less tied to their parties."[12]

Harold E. Hughes was ideally suited to this new era of issues and personalities. In his victorious 1962 campaign Hughes had been most outspoken on the question of liquor reform, but he had also embraced a broad program of progressive ideas, a program he presented to an Iowa public eager for change and discussion on these issues.

Hughes was endowed with natural abilities and assets which have benefited politicians in all times. A rugged, handsome man, he carried his massive six-foot, three-inch frame gracefully, spell-binding crowds with a deep, hypnotic voice. Hughes also held credentials collected from the common experiences of his state's culture, credentials that gained the respect of Iowa voters. In high school, he had been an all-state football player, state champion in the discus throw, and even all-state tuba player (a notable accomplishment in the home state of Karl King and Meredith

Willson). He had dropped out of college to fight in World War II, returning to Iowa to establish his own small trucking bureau.

In addition to his personal attributes, Hughes's fortunate access to prudent political counselors was an important key to his effective leadership. One man in particular—Park Rinard—ushered Harold Hughes into the limelight. An unusual personal background had prepared Park Rinard for his role in Iowa politics at a time when the state's rural past and urban future collided. A liberal, a highly articulate man, and a good writer, Rinard understood the basic sentiments of Iowans. He had acquired this sensitivity, in part, while serving as executive secretary and close friend to Iowa painter Grant Wood. Some years later, Rinard had joined the staff of Democratic Governor Herschel Loveless as administrative assistant. At that time, perhaps before anyone else, Rinard had recognized Harold Hughes's potential and strongly encouraged him to embark on a political career of his own—as a Democrat.

In his earliest political activities, Hughes was a Republican and had been elected delegate to several GOP state conventions. Subsequent personal frustrations with that party, however, and business conflicts between his own trucking bureau and the Republican-controlled Iowa State Commerce Commission, which regulated Iowa's trucking industry, had prompted Hughes to change his party affiliation. In 1958, with the encouragement and advice of Rinard and of Herschel Loveless, Hughes ran successfully for Commerce Commissioner as a Democrat. Two years later, Hughes made his first attempt for the Democratic gubernatorial nomination, but lost. Beginning with those initial campaigns, Rinard served as Hughes's principal strategist and advisor, and remained such until Hughes retired from political life in 1974.

DEMOCRATS REBORN

Although together Rinard and Hughes greatly influenced Iowa politics, their relationship was in itself largely invisible to Iowans. Throughout Hughes's tenure as governor, Rinard served not on the governor's staff but as head of an urban interest group called the League of Iowa Municipalities. From that post, Rinard conducted daily telephone deliberations with Hughes. For six years, from 1962 to 1968, while Rinard performed as the governor's closest confidant, he also acted as lobbyist for the League, advancing causes in the corridors of the statehouse which he had discussed and planned privately with Hughes.

Rinard's ability to interpret political matters both from the perspective of a grass-roots Iowan and from a progressive viewpoint shaped Hughes's own beliefs and political impulses. Edward Campbell, another aide close to Hughes, described the relationship:

Park was Harold Hughes's closest ally. He is the best political strategist in the state there is and one of the best writers in the country; and he has a tremendous grasp of the issues.... Such issues as equal rights, aid to parochial schools and riddance of the death penalty, as well as reapportionment, were his ideas along with Hughes's. And when Hughes would get turned down by the legislature, he would take it to the people and stump the state for support. None of these issues would have been in the forefront without the counsel of Park Rinard and none would have gone through without Harold Hughes out on the war path, waving the banner.... It was like the relationship of a songwriter and a vocalist, that type of team. It was about as unique a political marriage as you could find.[13]

With Rinard's counsel and polish, Hughes melded his own oratorical powers to address simply and forcefully the issues of the day. Iowans perceived in Hughes an uncommon sense of personal integrity and responded to Hughes's conviction that governmental action, properly conceived, and individual interest, unselfishly sacrificed, could join to re-establish bonds of community in the state.

A PARTY REBORN

In important and highly visible ways, Hughes exhibited a willingness to place his understanding of the general good above what seemed to be his natural inclinations. It seemed unusually bold and honest for an admitted alcoholic to desire repeal of the last vestiges of Prohibition from the State Code when many Iowans hovered in "key clubs" to do their drinking. As an avid hunter and gun-collector in a state filled with hunting enthusiasts, he increasingly advocated gun-control legislation. And himself a small-town native, he stormed through the state rallying forces to defeat the Shaff reapportionment plan as he advanced the cause of more equitable urban apportionment in the General Assembly. In many ways Hughes forced Iowans to assume a new integrity.

Hughes's unorthodox approach to politics and an enigmatic quality about his personality appealed to a wide variety of Iowans. As governor, he displayed characteristics and mannerisms not seen before in the chief executive's office. At times the restless and individualistic cowboy spirit that possessed him seemed more appropriate to his earlier vocation as truck driver than to his new position as head of the state government. He was, it seemed, instinctively more at ease hunting and fishing with a few old friends than working in the institutional confines of the governor's office. On one particularly intense day during his first term of office, Hughes sneaked out the back door of the State Capitol, walked to the Des Moines River, which runs through the middle of the city, and cast a fishing line over the guardrail of an avenue bridge.

Not just a roughly-hewn truck driver caught in a constricting bureaucracy, Hughes personified many of Iowa's essential cultural contradictions. Indeed, the novelist Vance Bourjaily, an Iowan and a personal friend of Hughes's, once wrote of him: "Governor Hughes is one of those men of balanced contradiction who sometimes occur in our political life.... It is as if... the checks and balances which our civics books speak of as being fundamental to the democratic structure were embodied in single human systems."[14] Of all the contradictions in Hughes's personality, the most pronounced involved his struggle to discover a religious identity amidst competing personal and spiritual impulses, a personal struggle he often confronted publicly through various religious endeavors.

As a young man, Hughes's wrenching combat experiences in World War II and the tragic automobile death of his older brother plunged him into a personal chaos for which his Methodist upbringing in Ida Grove had not adequately prepared him.[15] His youthful belief in a warm and friendly God was shattered. He recoiled from the torments of his doubts in a succession of alcoholic stupors over a ten-year period. "I couldn't understand a loving God allowing these things to happen," Hughes later recalled.[16] According to his own account, he even contemplated suicide. Instead, swearing off liquor, he committed himself to a renewed and transfigured Christian faith.

As a practicing politician in the decades following his spiritual rebirth, Hughes displayed enormous evangelical energy, attempting to save individual citizens and political peers from the torments of alcohol, drugs, and lives unredeemed.[17] But Hughes intertwined his message with a gospel reflecting his own profound desire to improve social conditions as well as individual souls. Hughes held out one hand to Iowa's agrarian, evangelical past, a history that included men and women who, like himself, were ruggedly spiritual and politically individualistic. With his other hand he grasped a line tied to a social-Christian tradition, desiring progressive, collective means to ease societal ills.

The often conflicting demands of evangelical and social

A PARTY REBORN

Christianity created a constant tension within Hughes. Sometimes he unnerved his fellow politicians when he left their meetings, both as governor and as senator, to assist ailing alcoholics and narcotics addicts who had requested his personal guidance. When he retired from his Senate seat in 1974 to devote himself to Christian laywork, Hughes stated his belief that his conflict was not resolvable through rational thought and action, but through faith alone:

> I've looked at this in every way. I've explored all these things you ask about. I know I have a responsibility to my family, staff, state, party, and nation. This decision affects all of them. But when I weighed it all, I knew that the Lord has directed my life until now; and he will use my life for a greater purpose. I can't explain it to you, but I have absolute faith that it is true.... I will be just as interested in social problems as I've ever been; I fail to see that this move will affect that.[18]

To seek religious and political reconcilation became the most salient theme of Harold Hughes's public career. That a man like Hughes, conscious of such deep fissures within himself, would lead many Iowans in their own search for a new community was startling. And yet, perhaps only such a person, riddled with many of the same tendencies and contradictions that troubled the state as a whole, could have had such a far-reaching impact upon Iowa politics in those years during which the state was transformed from a rural to an urban society.

As governor, Hughes stood in stark contrast to his indecisive predecessor. His whole-hearted advocacy of social reforms also differentiated him from former Governor Herschel Loveless, who was of a more conservative bent.[19] Speaking to an overwhelmingly Republican legislature in his first inaugural address, the new governor admonished: "It is sometimes said that the knack of skillful government is to stand back, do as little as possible, and make no mistakes. I hope there is another way—for between you and me, this prospect does not invite my soul."[20] Determined to introduce Iowa to a new era of progressive politics attentive to what he felt were the neglected needs of urban citizens, Hughes established the central theme of his first two years in office in that first speech to the legislature: "As I see it, we have no choice—if we are to keep faith with our oaths of office. Our constitution states that 'all political power is inherent in the people.'... The differences that divide us as partisans are small by comparison with the common ground that unites us as fellow Iowans."[21] Urban turf formed the common ground upon which Hughes built a bipartisan following. He pushed a wide range of social legislation before the General Assembly, the kind of laws urban legislators of both parties had promoted for nearly a decade, but which strongly entrenched rural interests had effectively resisted.

Largely due to the governor's leadership, party affiliation mattered less in the 60th General Assembly than in any session since World War II. Instead, urban-rural differences took precedence over partisan division on a wide range of issues, a marked change from the 1950s. From 1951 to 1955, only the reapportionment and butter-oleomargarine controversies managed to bring urban-rural differences to the surface; but in the 1963 session this division was evident in the battles over most major bills, many of which directly affected cities and towns. Cooperation between the Democrats and Republicans from urban counties brought substantive changes to Iowa law.[22]

Hughes led legislative breakthroughs in such areas as taxation formulas, reapportionment, public utility regulation, fair employment practices, and workmen's compensation increases. Nick Kotz, a Pulitzer Prize-winning reporter for the *Des Moines Register,* would look back in

A PARTY REBORN

1968 to the 60th General Assembly and call it a turning point in Iowa history.[23] Another veteran reporter, Frank T. Nye of the *Cedar Rapids Gazette,* concurred, having earlier labelled it perhaps "the best" session in Iowa history to date.[24]

But the public remembered the session not for such complex (though important) matters as taxation formulas. It was the repeal of the liquor-by-the-drink laws that caught the attention of the voters. Harold Hughes himself later observed: "Liquor by the drink was probably the least important thing I did, even if it is the most remembered."[25] But despite Hughes's comment, repeal was important because it symbolized a new political attitude in the state. The same Republican Party whose majorities had avoided the issue for more than a decade now publicly committed itself to change when prodded by Hughes. The Democratic Party, having carried through its most important platform pledges, now was demonstrably allied to progressive causes.

Hughes did suffer one major setback during the session, but even this he transformed into an ultimate boost to his party's progressive image. Over the governor's vociferous objections, the Republican majority approved, as had the previous General Assembly, the reapportionment constitutional amendment known as the Shaff Plan. As required by law, Iowa prepared for a special election to approve or to reject the amendment. Against great odds and the advice of Lex Hawkins and others predicting scenarios of the governor's humiliation, Hughes travelled across the state calling for the defeat of the amendment. Moderate and conservative Republicans joined with the IMA and IFBF to encourage its endorsement. In a surprising upset, in December 1963 Hughes and the urban forces defeated the Shaff Plan. One month later a Federal District Court

DEMOCRATS REBORN

directed the legislature to draw up two new reapportionment plans: a "temporary" plan to be used in the quickly approaching 1964 elections, and a "permanent" plan subject to the normal and lengthy amendment-approval procedures.[26] Even though the temporary plan increased urban representation, 47% of the electorate could still elect a majority of representatives while 39% could still elect a majority of senators.

THE 1962 GUBERNATORIAL VICTORY of Harold Hughes had been largely a personal one. He carried few other Democrats with him into office. The Republicans had captured 236 of 304 county offices, all state executive offices (except the governorship), six of seven congressional seats (Neal Smith was the lone Democratic winner), a United States Senate seat, as well as the vast majority of the seats in the General Assembly.[27]

To a large extent, Republican successes had resulted from habitual voting patterns of Iowa's citizens. Also important, however, had been the Democratic Party's lack of tactical and organizational expertise outside of Polk County. In 1962 neither of Iowa's political parties exhibited much sophisticated political professionalism, but the Demcrats remained particularly amateurish. Sometimes this inexperience, combined with shortages of money, forced Democratic candidates into absurd and distracting predicaments. E. B. Smith's 1962 campaign for United States Senate vividly demonstrated such organizational difficulties. It contrasted sharply with the more thoroughly organized campaigns the Democrats would launch in the 1970s.

E. B. Smith, a professor of history at Iowa State University in Ames, captured his party's nomination for the U.S. Senate in a unique way. Many active Democrats had assumed Congressman Merwin Coad, first elected from north-central Iowa's Sixth District in 1956, would be the party's obvious candidate to oppose three-term incumbent Republican Bourke Hickenlooper. But Coad, a former minister from Boone, demolished his own political credibility when he become embroiled in widely publicized marriage, gambling, and legislative scandals in Washington. Into the unexpected political void left by Coad, Lex Hawkins and other party leaders thrust the startled Professor Smith, an Iowa resident of fewer than five years. Suddenly he found himself in the spotlight of the Democratic state convention and a statewide campaign.[28]

Nominated in unorthodox fashion, E. B. Smith proceeded to campaign that way as well. Supported only by an unpaid campaign staff of three and a budget of less than $25,000, Smith needed a cheap, effective way to gain publicity. He joined most of the other statewide Democratic candidates (with the exception of Hughes) as they piled into a rented Greyhound bus and travelled in a caravan over 3,000 miles in 14 days. In the end, the men on the bus found the caravan tactic to lack political genius. As Tom Dawson, a Smith campaign aide, recalls:

> The caravan experiment was very loosely planned because nobody had considered the problem of scheduling. At that time, there was no such thing as a "scheduler." So, the first day out in the field we were all filled with great inspiration—the whole ticket, less Hughes, piled into the bus....
> And the bus was never on the "schedule" that was planned. Sometimes, as we would drive along one of the candidates would yell from the back of the bus, "Hey, my uncle Elmer lives just down that road a few miles, and he'd be terribly upset if we didn't stop to say hello." So the bus would turn down the side roads and we'd visit with all the Uncle Elmers.
> I remember one stop along the road that turned into a fiasco. At Keokuk, someone had planned a "mass rally." Of course, nobody among the Democrats down there had the experience in planning large rallies. So we arrived in the middle of an immense field where the rally

DEMOCRATS REBORN

was supposed to be. But nobody showed up. And Hughes arrived in his car. Well, there was nothing we could do, so we started to play football on that large, empty field. Then we went downtown, loaded out of the bus and sat through the afternoon in a hotel lobby. There was nobody to talk to.[29]

The final blow to E. B. Smith's campaign demonstrated the problem created by the absence of strong Democratic leaders in Iowa with power at the national level. During the crucial weeks of the campaign, Hickenlooper, the ranking Republican member of the Senate Foreign Affairs Committee, was frequently called back to Washington to confer personally with President John F. Kennedy on such important matters as the Cuban missile crisis. Apparently insensitive to Smith's campaign efforts, Kennedy labelled Hickenlooper "one of his most trusted advisors" on national security issues, making it difficult for Smith either to accuse the Senator of ineptitude or to assert his own superior qualifications for the office.[30]

Though burdened by the inherent difficulties of running an organized and under-financed campaign, Smith proved to be a formidable and energetic candidate. An experienced public speaker with a quick wit, he covered the state making speeches and, for the first time in Iowa politics, he used television to promote his campaign through a series of telethons. In the end, against all odds, the professor pulled himself to the threshold of victory, only to be defeated by less than a 2% margin of the total vote.[31]

Even while E. B. Smith lived through his campaign ordeal, other Democrats had begun desperately working to fulfill their own dreams of a statewide grass-roots party organization. The heat of the 1960 and 1962 election campaigns forged a strong alliance between the Democrats and labor (particularly the United Auto Workers), an alliance that, in turn, buttressed Democratic organizational efforts in many of Iowa's urban areas.

A PARTY REBORN

In the 1960 campaign, for the first time ever, locals of the 9,000-strong UAW placed several of their own members on salary to help register other union people to vote. Then, on election day, the UAW paid nearly 100 members to walk the streets of urban areas and to draw sympathetic voters to the polls.[32] In 1962 the UAW and the state Democratic Party institutionalized their relationship when the party hired UAW leader Edris "Soapy" Owens, who had grown frustrated with the lack of political activism in the state's AFL-dominated AFL-CIO, as its first executive secretary.[33]

In the meantime, State Chairman Lex Hawkins had brought zeal and energy to the organizational efforts of the Democrats. Described by Soapy Owens as someone "who would walk on his mother's spine to win an election," Hawkins moved to build up party structures in the state's most populous counties and to widen the financial and political base of the state party Central Committee. "I did not take on the state chairman's job to win a popularity contest," Hawkins declared. "I'm out to organize the Democratic Party in Iowa."[34] The Polk County organization, which in 1962 alone jumped Democratic voter registrations from an evenly matched race with the Republicans to a lead of nearly 7,000 registered voters, continued to serve as the model for Hawkins' nuts-and-bolts politics. "All I have done is to present the same program on a statewide basis that we have been using in Polk County," the Chairman said as he asked congressional district meetings across Iowa for an unprecedented financial war chest of $300,000 to underwrite 1962 campaign costs. "The Republicans spend that much. We never have. All I am trying to do is be realistic about what it will take to win."[35]

The Republicans may have been spending as much

DEMOCRATS REBORN

money as Hawkins claimed they were, but the GOP was suffering. The liberal-conservative battles once fought only within its own ranks now were being fought between the political parties as well. Republican State Chairman Robert D. Ray, an attorney from Polk County and, at 34, the youngest person ever to head either political party in Iowa, responded to the increasingly successful method of his Democratic counterparts.[36] Ray called for better party organization and an end to the "hands-off" policies of the 1950s. He denounced his party for being "too timid and too late," and for not having taken strong stands on controversial issues such as reapportionment and liquor-by-the-drink.[37] Not unlike Leo Hoegh a decade earlier, Ray attempted to realign his party with the urban areas and also tried to disassociate it from the tight grip of interest groups. Ray appointed H. Rand Peterson as campaign chairman of the GOP, and Peterson expressed the Ray plan for a new Republican urban insurgency. "I welcome the challenge that now confronts the Iowa Republican Party, especially that the party return to a proper perspective of the city voter and make sure he understands Republican principles, which are essential to the long range welfare of the cities," Peterson said.[38]

A little later, when told that the IFBF and the IMA did not agree with him about reapportionment, Ray said he was not about to try to please special interest groups. Like progressive Republicans before him, the new state chairman found many members of his own party hesitated to follow his lead. Because over 60% of Iowa's Republicans opposed Barry Goldwater's candidacy for president, Ray refused to back the Arizona senator at the 1964 Republican National Convention, holding ten of Iowa's 24-member delegation in support of moderate William Scranton of Pennsylvania. Conservative party members and interest groups roundly criticized Ray for this, even as the urban press applauded him.[39]

Facing the 1964 elections, then, the Democrats did so from a posture of increasing strength, confronting a Republican Party torn by internal divisions. The presidential candidacy of Lyndon Johnson further enhanced the Democrats' progressive image cultivated by Harold E. Hughes in his first term as governor. In 1962 Lex Hawkins had prophesied, "Democrats may not win the state offices in two years, but in four to six years Iowa will be Democratic." His prophesy now served as inspirational dogma for party workers.[40]

When Iowa joined the 1964 Johnson landslide and an unusually large number of Democrats won state offices, electoral totals confirmed the general impression that 1963 had been a watershed year (see Figure 1). Iowans were voting for Democrats with increased frequency,[41] and more importantly, a larger number of them identified themselves as Democrats.[42]

In 1964 six of seven Democrats running for Congress defeated their Republican opponents. Only the cantankerous and conservative H. R. Gross of the Third District now held a seat for the Republicans. Among the Democrats John C. Culver of the Second District joined veteran Neal Smith in Washington, D.C.; a few years later, Culver would play a critical role in enlarging and refining the statewide party organization. In the gubernatorial race, Hughes doubled Johnson's margin of victory over Goldwater, winning an astounding 68% of the vote against moderate Republican challenger Evan Hultman.[43]

Democrats also won control of both houses of the state legislature for the first time in 30 years. They now held 100 of 124 House seats and 34 of 59 Senate positions in a legislature newly expanded in size by the temporary reappor-

DEMOCRATS REBORN

Gubernatorial candidate Harold E. Hughes, 1960 (right); Lex Hawkins (bottom left) and Park Rinard (bottom right) in 1960

tionment plan. This increased Democratic strength derived substantially from the 25 additional seats assigned to the state's most populous counties. Polk County's House delegation, for instance, increased from two to eleven members, and the same county had three senators rather than one—all Democrats. Youthfulness marked the new legislature. No freshman member was over 48 years old, and 100 of the 183 members were new. Probably no session since the first General Assembly in 1846 could have claimed less political experience. In addition, significantly fewer farmers and more blue-collar workers served in this session of the legislature than in any session since the close of World War II.[44]

The members of the 61st General Assembly (1965) desired reform, but they were flexible as to what shape they might give to change. From the very start, Hughes and his associates did much of the molding. Hughes startled members of both parties when he announced his preference for the House speakership, New Hampton Democrat Vincent Steffen. Hughes's action was an unprecedented gubernatorial move in Iowa politics, since legislators had always considered the speakership appointment to be a privilege of the majority party, an internal matter to be settled without interference from the executive branch. Lex Hawkins delivered a shock of his own when, at a House Democratic caucus, he argued for the choice Hughes had made. House Democrats finally agreed to the Hughes decision. In the Senate, the shrewd and newly elected Democratic Lieutenant Governor Robert Fulton, also Hughes's personal choice, presided. Unlike the preceding session when Hughes had seemingly acted alone, the governor now strongly tied the 1965 General Assembly to his own will. This proved effective, and the session accomplished more than any other since that of 1846.

DEMOCRATS REBORN

The 1965 General Assembly passed eight proposed constitutional amendments. In over a century, no other single session had passed as many. The eight amendments dealt with a variety of issues, legalizing bingo games, apportioning the legislature by a new formula (the "permanent" plan designed to conform with the U.S. Supreme Court's one-man, one-vote decision), scheduling annual sessions of the legislature, and teaming candidates for governor and lieutenant governor on party tickets.

In addition to the constitutional amendments, the legislators unleashed a flood of new laws that rural Republicans had dammed behind committee doors for nearly a decade. In the most notable of these new laws, members abolished capital punishment, created a state withholding tax, imposed limits on interstate highway billboards, increased appropriations for state aid to schools by one-half, increased agricultural land-tax credits to help relieve property taxes, authorized 16 comprehensive combined area community colleges and vocational schools as well as four new vocational-technical training schools, permitted county supervisors to create the office of public defender, increased workmen's compensation and employment security benefits, initiated penal reforms, revamped guidelines for secondary education in the state, and adopted daylight savings time.

Hughes promoted "Great Society" attitudes towards taxes and social services. Whereas earlier governors had often denied the need for increased tax rates or had proposed to increase regressive sales taxes, Hughes supported new and primarily progressive taxes that would finance the broadened social service legislation. With the governor's prodding, legislators increased the state income tax rate levied upon higher income brackets and boosted taxes on cigarettes, on gasoline, and on inheritances.[45]

A PARTY REBORN

The legislative foundation laid in the 1965 session transformed Iowa's political dialogue. Political leaders of the future would talk about streamlining and improving the administration of the Hughes program, but not even conservative Republicans would talk of abolishing it.

THE CUMULATIVE IMPACT of this legislation was both dramatic and long-lasting. However, the most spectacular moments of Hughes's second term involved more than legislation. Hughes engaged himself in two highly emotional battles. Both conflicts pointed to the sometimes excruciating tension still existing between Iowa's rural past and its urban future, between the state's one-party political tradition and a new era when interest groups competed within a viable two-party system.

In the first battle Governor Hughes helped to form a compromise between the Old Order Amish and residents of two northeast Iowa communities. The dispute centered on the education of Amish children. Hughes plunged into the local tangle and used his own power and influence to lead Iowans to reconsider their treatment of non-conforming minority groups, to ponder their relationship to rural customs of the past, and to strike a new balance between civil law and social justice.

In the second fight, Hughes squared off to face the "right-to-work" issue. For two decades it had pitted the state's labor movement against Iowa's business leaders. When Hughes entered the fray, he demanded difficult compromises from members of his own personal following and from the political parties themselves.

His actions and the responses of Iowans to them highlighted important qualities of the state's political milieu. The positions taken by various groups and factions on the issues now superceded partisan loyalties. The tower-

DEMOCRATS REBORN

ing importance of those issues held the promise of creating formidable new political alliances within parties as well as the imminent threat of sudden party disintegration.

On the brisk morning of Friday, November 19, 1965 a yellow school bus, packed with school officials from Oelwein and Hazleton communities, drove along its planned route, from one Amish farm to the next. Truant Officer Owen Snively stepped out at each of those farms long enough to announce to the Amish parents he intended to take their children aboard the bus and transport them to the Hazleton schools. At each stop Snively returned to the bus empty-handed. Wary parents had hidden their children well in advance of Snively's arrival. Still, the officials continued their journey. Now accompanied by a caravan of 17 carloads of news reporters and onlookers, the bus finally arrived at Amish School Number One, or the "South School," and Snively once more stepped off the bus, this time with Hazleton Sheriff Fred Beier. The two men entered the white one-room building, and Truant Officer Snively interrupted the Amish children in class. He told them they would have to come with him to Hazleton. The students, boys in broad-brimmed hats and girls in black shawls and bonnets, all in dark clothing, lined up single file without protest and walked towards the bus. Then suddenly somebody shouted in German, "Run!"

The group quickly scattered, some to the dusty road nearby, others over the fence bordering the schoolyard and into adjacent cornfields. Most escaped, but the attending officers caught a few. Emanuel Borntreger, 13 years old, arms held by a deputy sheriff, broke into tears. They found Sara Schmucker, only six, terrified, shivering, and in hysterics, in the cornfield. Oelwein Superintendent of Schools Arthur Sensor, himself sobbing, escorted Sara to a nearby car.[46]

A PARTY REBORN

The reporters and photographers captured the tragic moment from every angle. They wired their stories across the nation, and an intensely bitter three-year local conflict had escalated beyond the capacity of the area's citizens to resolve it. Governor Hughes was now prepared to intervene. He later expressed sentiments no doubt shared by many Iowans: "I'm not going to be critical of people who are trying to uphold the law which they have sworn to protect. But that doesn't keep me from having compassion in my heart for people who believe so strongly in their faith that they are willing to sacrifice everything."[47]

The conflict over the Amish schools became the most extreme and poignant demonstration of Iowa's difficulty in adjusting to an entirely new era of living and working and thinking. Even people not directly affected by the school issue became involved emotionally because they themselves had come from a past largely at variance with their present circumstances. Many Iowans understood that here among the gentlest of the state's people, jet-age rules and regulations threatened to crush a horse-and-buggy culture. They sympathized with the white-bearded, silken-haired old men, clad in overalls, who quoted Biblical scripture in response to the obtuse, technical legalities read to them by government officials wearing polyester suits. And for those who understood and sympathized, the calls of local citizens and many Iowans to provide universal education and equal opportunity to all children in the modern world—by force if necessary—fell on ears seeking to hear the sounds of the past. The clatter of horses' hooves and the crunch of metal-rimmed buggy wheels headed home along gravel roads reminded many older Iowans of their former days. Even those now adjusted to city life, people who had once attended one-room school houses, recalled the wrenching sense of loss they themselves had experienced when their own community school districts had been expanded and consolidated to include other towns and cities. It was an experience broadly shared by Iowans. Many remembered a time in their own past when unique pocket communities had abounded, waiting to be discovered. They now looked with mixed feelings at the postwar era of unceasing mobility and ubiquitous communications networks, at its televisions, its telephones, its superhighways, its airports, at all those things threatening to homogenize every aspect of life.

Harold Hughes's response to the Amish school conflict demonstrated his intuitive ability to lead his state in this difficult transition. Hughes reminded Iowans, even in the failing and unpopular compromises he offered, that traditional values could be as useful in the new age as in the old. Through his actions the governor showed Iowans that, in the life of a person or a state, one era need not be totally dismissed to benefit from the rise of another.

At issue in the Amish school controversy was whether or not every school in the state must comply completely with state education laws. Officials of the recently consolidated Oelwein and Hazleton school district, insisting on the letter of the law, contended Amish children must attend regular public schools and be instructed by state-certified teachers. For the intimidated Amish, attendance at urban public schools promised not only an end to their specific teachings (which, for example, did not include instruction in the sciences), but also a disturbance of their distinctive rural way of life. More than a legal dispute, in several years' time the controversy had escalated into a breakdown of communications between the Amish and their neighbors, hampering all efforts at reconciliation. As Harold Hughes emphasized:

The Amish school dispute arises from one of the most difficult problems

A PARTY REBORN

of communication ever encountered in Iowa. On the one hand, you have a devout people whose religion requires them to live in accordance with old ways and customs. On the other hand, you have a modern society whose educational system is based on the proposition that all children have an equal right to be taught by properly qualified teachers.[48]

Actually, the seeds of the difficulty had been planted nearly 20 years earlier. Before 1947, the two Hazleton Amish school houses now embroiled in the dispute had been public institutions. But when the Hazleton Consolidated School District had been created that year, the Amish recoiled from sending their children to the consolidated public schools. Instead, they purchased two abandoned one-room schoolhouses and paid for private instruction while also paying property taxes to support the Hazleton public schools.

In the years that followed, many people wanted to consolidate further, making Hazleton and Oelwein, its larger neighbor, one school district. Consolidation, its advocates claimed, would improve the quality of education while decreasing school costs. The proposal was highly popular in Oelwein, but in Hazleton a forceful group opposed consolidation plans, fearing their own town would be dominated by its larger neighbor. In 1961, when Oelwein school officials pushed for the additional Hazleton-Oelwein consolidation, they sought the support of the Amish community and discussed the possible effects of such a move with the Old Order leaders. As a result of these talks, and with the express approval of Paul Johnston, Iowa's state superintendent of schools, the Amish were promised they could continue to use their own schoolhouses. The informal agreement stipulated the new consolidated district would provide, at public expense, certified teachers who would adapt their teachings to the desires of the Old Order Amish. With this understanding,

DEMOCRATS REBORN

Governor Harold Hughes with legislative leaders, 1964 (above); with presidential candidate Eugene McCarthy, 1968 (below left); and with an Amish elder, 1966 (below right)

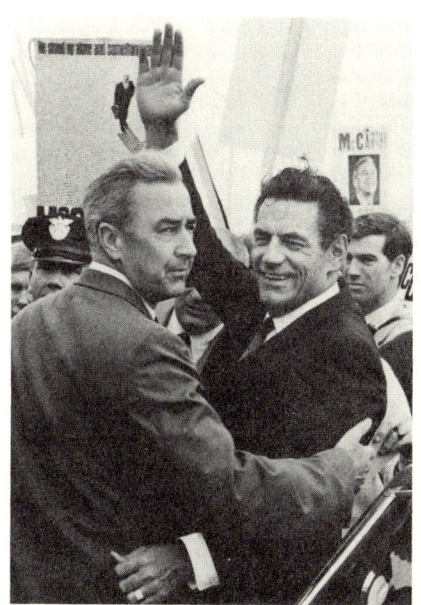

the Old Order leaders supported the consolidation vote in the November election, a vote still heavily opposed by other Hazleton residents. When the voters narrowly approved the new district plan, many Hazleton residents were enraged. Not one Hazleton school board member had won election to the new board, and the longstanding Hazleton fears of being overwhelmed by Oelwein seemed fully justified.

Believing the Amish to be responsible for the election results because of the agreement made between their leaders and the Oelwein officials, Hazleton residents became bitter toward their Amish neighbors. Fed by the new resentments, their intolerance for the peculiar habits of the Old Order residents increased. The Amish had protected their own community's schools, while Hazleton residents had lost theirs to the consolidation efforts. Tensions grew, and Hazleton citizens pushed the new school board to force the Amish to give up their unique status. The consolidated district needed funds to expand school facilities, and to gain voter support for the upcoming bond elections Oelwein officials sought the support of the angered Hazleton residents. Toward that end, in May of 1962, the new school board reneged on its informal agreement with the Amish. Now, the board said curriculum would *not* be adjusted to the wishes of the Old Order elders. Now the board called the use of the one-room schools a *temporary* plan, to be followed in the future by full Amish attendance at public schools. Two days after the board made these announcements, and without prior consultation with Amish leaders, the state superintendent of schools sent an inspection team to the one-room buildings. The inspectors found the schools' physical condition unacceptable. Following the announcements and the inspection, the bond issue enjoyed the support of both communities—if not the Amish—and passed easily.

The sudden reversal of events, the shattering of agreements, and the unanticipated inspection shocked the Amish, and the Old Order decided to defy state law. In the fall of 1962, they reopened their schools, employing their own non-certified teachers. From that point until the famed cornfield chase in 1965, the Amish and the county superintendent of schools engaged in a running battle. Amish parents were often fined for the truancy of their children from the public schools. When they refused to pay, they had been jailed, liens had been filed on their property, and their crops had been sold to take care of the fines.

Animosities deepened. The Amish question dominated all other local political issues. The citizens of Oelwein and Hazleton elected a school board filled with people less willing to compromise with the Amish. With the number of incidents mounting between the Plain People and the public, County Attorney Harlan Lemon invited Iowa Attorney General Lawrence Scalise to contribute to the resolution of the problem. But Scalise failed to find middle ground between the groups. Finally, in the last of a long series of episodes, the school board decided to force the Amish to attend public schools by using charges of truancy to pull children out of the one-room schools and into the urban consolidated classrooms. In this highly charged atmosphere, school officials launched the first truancy roundup on the morning of November 19, 1965, sparking a national outcry of sympathy for the plight of the Amish.

Governor Hughes tried to cool the heated passions. He called for a moratorium on levying further truancy charges. Only past court costs and fines, Hughes said, would be held against the Amish, although Hughes later remitted $8,000 owed to the state.[49]

Two months later, on January 10, 1966, the governor

flew to Oelwein to meet with the Old Order leaders, to speak to Oelwein public school students, and to confer with the Oelwein school board. He went first to the home of Amish leader Dan Borntreger, where he spoke for two hours with nine elders, trying to find avenues of compromise. Then he visited one of the two Amish schoolhouses near Hazleton, accompanied by Andy Kaufman, an Amish parent who had personally accumulated over $500 in truancy fines. Without speaking, Hughes quietly observed the students. When Hughes left the schoolhouse, he passed an American flag flying upside-down, the international signal for times of distress. News photographers wired a picture of Hughes and the flag across the nation.[50]

Hughes balanced the attention he paid to the special needs of the Old Order with a statement he made to public school students at the Oelwein junior high school. There, he embraced the values shared by most Iowans, the beliefs most threatened by Amish separatism: "We must respect the right of others to live differently...if it is an honest and decent way of life." But he also noted that, "every student should have the opportunity to develop to the maximum of his ability....none should be abandoned."[51] The governor's remarks went to the heart of the controversy. They recognized the need for a modern society to enforce uniformly its statutes—in this case, Iowa's compulsory education law—while also respecting diversity and the Amish desire to remain religiously isolated from that modern society.[52] Hughes ended his day in Oelwein with the school board members, again seeking compromises and hoping to create a new atmosphere of understanding.

In a month's time, Hughes, back at the Capitol, worked out a temporary compromise proposal. The governor planned to use a $15,000 grant from the Danforth Foundation to pay certified teachers for two years to instruct the

Amish children in accordance with general Old Order educational practices. Under Hughes's proposal the Oelwein public school district would rent the two schoolhouses for $1 per year, thereby making them public, not parochial, schools. In addition, Hughes hoped, the German language, but not religion, would be taught in the classes. Neither a science curriculum nor the use of modern teaching aides, such as movies or television, would be required. According to the governor's plan, the Amish must agree to abide by state law in such matters as compulsory attendance. Coupling this short-term proposal with a long-range initiative, Hughes proposed legislation to create an annual $50,000 "supplemental aid" education fund to finance solutions to unique problems in the state, like the current Amish school situation.

Hughes returned to Oelwein on February 15, 1966 to present his compromise to the Amish elders. In an environment filled with symbols pointing to fundamental differences between the parties involved in the conflict, the governor once again flew down in his private plane and was sped by auto to the center of Oelwein. There, a block off Main Street, in the cinder-block hall of the Friar Watson American Legion Post, Hughes met with the religious leaders who had arrived in their horse-drawn buggies. Dan Borntreger and his Old Order companions accepted the Hughes plan, and the governor returned to Des Moines to lobby his new bill. In time, Hughes also convinced the Oelwein and Hazleton school officials to follow his lead.

But the governor stood to lose support both from Iowa citizens and the legislature for his advocacy of Amish rights. The *Fayette County Union,* hearing the details of the Hughes plan, offered its own critique: "Most of us had the impression old Dan [Borntreger] came away from the bargaining table with everything but Governor Hughes's

A PARTY REBORN

Congressman John C. Culver, after winning his first election, 1964 (below), and campaigning for re-election, 1966 (above).

suspenders. Now it would appear he wanted them too."⁵³ The governor also discovered stiff opposition to his proposal among legislators. Many objected to the possibly unconstitutional precedent set by the plan. Might there be later calls for general state support of other parochial and private schools? Hughes responded to the charge by pointing out that the $1 per year rental arrangement defined the Amish schools as public, not private, institutions. Other critics complained the Amish compromise ran counter to the state's philosophy of consolidating school districts to improve the quality of education. Kenneth Wells, executive secretary of the Iowa State Education Association, said the maintenance of the one-room schools failed to follow "the whole trend of school reorganization.... I cannot see how this is a step forward at all."⁵⁴ The governor answered that the schools essentially would be forced to conform to state school standards. Finally, the Oelwein plan symbolized to some an unhealthy trend of catering to demands from factional groups at the expense of the state's wider community. Hughes's supporters directly dismissed these comments because they saw in such complaints a prejudice against minority groups veiled by legalisms. "We don't have many Negroes in the state so we pick on the Amish. We must not forget that society is made up of minority groups," declared Representative Mary Pat Gregerson, a Democrat from Council Bluffs.⁵⁵

The governor's compromise faced certain defeat in the legislature. A *Des Moines Register* poll revealed that of the 25 legislators most involved in matters of education, five favored the Hughes plan, eighteen opposed it, and only two had yet to decide.⁵⁶ Politicians eager for the governor's seat challenged Hughes's approach to the Amish school question in the 1966 gubernatorial campaign. "Governor Hughes's suggestion that the legislature should make a separate appropriation for this one group is unrealistic, and sets a dangerous precedent that would, in due time, become untenable," said one Republican candidate, Robert K. Beck. William G. Murray, another Republican hopeful from Ames, differed with Hughes and promised: "If elected governor and no permanent solution has been found, I plan to appoint a commission made up of leaders of all groups concerned" to settle the issue.[57]

Hughes lost the first attempt to have his plan approved by the General Assembly, but he won re-election to his third term as governor over candidate Murray. Following his victory, the governor borrowed his opponent's proposal and established an advisory committee to examine the problem. Later he sponsored the committee's recommendation to provide exemptions from the state's school-standards laws to the Amish and to allow the Amish to run their schools using any teachers they desired, so long as the Old Order children were able to pass periodic tests prescribed by the state superintendent of public instruction.[58] After some debate, less heated than a year before, on the last day of June, 1967, Governor Hughes signed the bill into law and closed an agonizing chapter of Iowa's history.

No single issue, no one event, defines the image or sets the tone for a political figure. But the Amish school controversy cast a revealing light on both Hughes and the state he served. Unafraid of immersing himself, and therefore his office, in the political miasma of local bitterness and conflict in order to face hard questions about significant problems affecting all Iowans, Hughes showed himself capable of acting from emotional and cultural, not merely political, impulses. By acting on such impulses, as he would again years later in his stand against the Vietnam War, Hughes ran counter to the conventional wisdom of

DEMOCRATS REBORN

political expediency. But in his leadership, amid the passions and the anger of a local feud that dealt with immediate and specific grievances, Hughes asked larger questions and directed the state's attention to its most crucial cultural concerns. Did nonconformity have a place in American life? Could inconvenient rural customs be preserved in Iowa's collective rush to the city? How great was Iowa's need to protect minority rights from the state's postwar increase in potential spirit-crushing power and influence? Could Iowans temper respect for the rule of law with simple acts of charity?

That Iowans answered these questions affirmatively during the Amish school crisis marked the intuitive, very personal bond between Hughes and his public. That Hughes would act on that bond revealed the secret of how he helped to change the very nature of his Iowa constituency during his career as governor.

WHILE STRUGGLING with the Amish school question, Harold E. Hughes also faced his most strenuous gubernatorial political difficulty within the Democratic Party. The matter concerned the issue of "right-to-work" laws. Ever since 1947, when the Iowa Manufacturers Association had helped to push through the state's controversial and stringent labor laws, unions had worked for their repeal. After their unsuccessful repeal efforts in the 1959 session of the General Assembly, labor leaders had concentrated much of their legislative attention on the reapportionment question, hoping greater urban representation would lead to the election of more Democrats and to an eventual revocation of the right-to-work laws. Not surprisingly, these labor leaders had been among Harold Hughes's strongest allies in his successful effort to defeat the Shaff Plan at the polls in December 1963.

A PARTY REBORN

The continued importance of the right-to-work laws in Iowa politics puzzled some citizens because many union shops existed in the state despite the statutes.[59] But it was a highly emotional issue, a symbol not only for the unions but for the IMA and the IFBF as well. The groups' long history of conflict blinded each to the possibility of compromise, and leaders of all three groups demanded resolution through outright legislative battle.

Labor leaders looked to the promise of a Democratic sweep in 1964 to assure the repeal of the labor statutes. At the state convention that year, apparently without the knowledge or approval of Hughes himself, labor sympathizers had written into the Democratic platform a plank that read: "...the Democratic Party of Iowa recommends action to repeal the so-called right-to-work law."[60]

The intransigence of labor put Hughes in an awkward position. He sympathized with labor's intent, yet he knew three-fourths of the state's citizens favored retention of the labor laws. Polls showed that even a majority of those who called themselves "laborers" supported the right-to-work laws.[61] In other words, while Hughes did favor the legalization of union shop contracts, it was, as Park Rinard recalls, "a political fact of life" that the governor could not advocate outright repeal of the labor laws.[62] As a result, Hughes groped for middle ground. On the one hand, he hoped not to betray the trust of labor or the intent of the convention. On the other hand, the governor tried desperately to keep intact the new and tenuous bonds among businessmen, farmers, and his administration. To make matters more difficult, Hughes himself was uncertain about the nature and impact of the laws in question and at first seemed confused about some of their basic provisions.

The ensuing battle between the governor and labor

DEMOCRATS REBORN

proved the Republican Party alone did not suffer from internal strife. As the Democrats broadened their base, they also increased their vulnerability to dissension among the ranks. But unlike the Republicans, the Democrats had a strong and dynamic leader in Hughes, a leader who could force compromises, mitigate bitter emotions, and prevent the fate of deep-seated factionalism that often plagued only entrenched parties like the Iowa Republicans.

As the legislative session opened, the governor tried to explain what had now become his delicate position. Despite the state Democratic platform, which specifically called for repeal of the right-to-work laws, Hughes proposed legalizing union shops through "modification"—not repeal—of the laws. The battle lines formed immediately. Baffled and outraged, the eleven Democratic Polk County Representatives introduced their own bill, supported by labor, calling for outright abolition of the statutes. Lieutenant Governor Robert Fulton later remarked of the controversy:

Labor, of course, was very influential with the Democrats and, in 1965, we had a knock-down, drag-out fight over who was going to run the party: the Governor and the party organization or the labor halls. It was very heated, and at one time a vice-president of the AFL-CIO told me that I'd never hold office again. At that time, all urban areas elected their officials at-large, and that allowed the unions much greater political leverage in the urban delegations for they could put their efforts to work in behalf of all the candidates they wanted.[63]

As fuzzy as Hughes attempted to make the battle lines appear, opponents pointedly attacked him from many sides. AFL-CIO chief Vern L. Davis continued to criticize the governor for diverging from the official Democratic platform plank.[64] Republican Party Chairman Robert Ray attempted his own explanation of Hughes's strategy, saying, "I think what is happening here is that in order to pacify all elements, the governor has taken a position both for

A PARTY REBORN

business and for labor by trying to lead people to believe you can have both the right-to-work law and the union shop at the same time. That, of course, is impossible."65 To salvage his fragile coalition, Hughes, in a stunning initiative, attended a Democratic caucus accompanied by Lieutenant Governor Fulton and Lex Hawkins. The governor pleaded with Democrats to put aside the labor issue and to pass as many of their less controversial platform pledges as possible. Then Hughes again promised he would work to legalize the union shop through modification rather than repeal of the right-to-work laws.66

In a month's time, Hughes convinced labor leaders to formulate a compromise agreement which would, in effect, nullify the state labor law. The agreement called for legalizing union shop and agency shop contracts, but did not require repeal of the labor statute. But when the bill came before the Senate, Republicans and rural Democrats reacted with overwhelming hostility, and Fulton instigated a move to defer action, avoiding certain defeat.67

In this climate, Harold Hughes made what Park Rinard has since labelled "the big speech which never received the recognition it deserved."68 Hughes called the legislature into an unusual joint session (rarely before had a governor called the full body together in mid-session) to announce his administration would shortly present a series of bills to revamp entirely the state's labor laws. One bill, Hughes said, would call for the legalization of the union shop. "Either we believe in collective bargaining or we do not. To me, this is the point on which it all hinges," Hughes declared. "The fair resolution of this issue will have an all-important bearing on the economic development and spiritual unity of this state in the years ahead." The legislature should grant labor "the dignity of fair partnership in the industry and business future of Iowa...instead of treating

DEMOCRATS REBORN

them as a distrusted and ill-favored stepchild."[69]

Following his dramatic speech, Hughes once again attended the Democratic caucus to plan strategy and to elicit support from rural members of the party. But his attempts failed to avert the defeat of his proposal by a 31-27 margin in the Senate, a defeat made possible by the votes of seven Democrats who joined the Republican opposition.[70]

The labor law struggle affected the Democratic Party in two important ways. First, it demonstrated that Hughes and his party did not intend to bow to the demands and ultimatums of any single group, even organized labor. Yet the Democrats had kept the labor groups as allies. Labor now looked to its own national organizations instead of the Iowa Democratic Party to work for repeal of Section 14-B of the Taft-Hartley Act. The bond between labor and the Iowa Democrats continued to exist, but only because of a mutual concern to advance a broader range of social and political issues.[71]

The second major result of the conflict proved more divisive for the Democrats, ultimately embroiling Harold E. Hughes and Lex Hawkins in their first and last public skirmish. The underlying predicament had become this: how should the party be structured, and how powerful should the party organization be in its effort to increase Democratic victories and assure candidate loyalties?

As state chairman, Hawkins had always advocated building powerful party organizations. When the seven Democratic senators had refused to support the Hughes-labor compromise, Hawkins sought to coerce them into greater responsiveness to the party by writing a new party constitution. Hawkins's charter called for formal party endorsements of primary candidates, obviously a tactic to increase the power of the state organization and to limit the importance of popular primaries.

A PARTY REBORN
— 114 —

In seeking support for his constitution, Hawkins assured party workers that party officials would not be able to abuse the new powers assigned them. Unconvinced, Harold Hughes instantly voiced objections to the endorsement scheme. Had such a plan been in effect when he first ran for office, the governor claimed, he never would have been governor because party regulars in those early years had never given him active support. Hughes felt that the plan was not in the best interest of the Democratic Party or of the people of Iowa. "I think this would be a mistake," he asserted. "It would take the nominations away from the rank and file and put them in the so-called smoke-filled rooms." Hughes insisted that the primary election should result in the nomination of people who represented the wishes of the majority of the party, not just the wishes of the party organization.[72]

Hawkins countered that candidates under the existing primary system were chosen in a smoke-filled room, the governor's office itself:

> The primary elections may have been wide-open in theory in 1964, but actually the governor and I sat down together and decided who would run for what offices. We don't have to do that anymore, and I don't think we ought to. The people who are going to have to work for these candidates in the fall ought to have the authority to say who is going to run. And I think the best way to do it is to let the representatives at the convention decide who will be the candidates.[73]

As the convention and upcoming debate on the new constitution approached, Hawkins forced Hughes to compromise. Together they decided that if no one candidate received more than two-thirds of the vote at the convention, the party could endorse more than one candidate. At the governor's insistence, they agreed that a convention could decide not to endorse any candidates for any office if those in attendance so desired.[74]

DEMOCRATS REBORN

In the midst of the battle with the governor, Hawkins surprisingly announced he would be retiring from his position after the state convention. By all indications, most delegates came to the Des Moines convention site prepared to side with Hughes. On the eve of the convention, Hawkins and his successor as chairman, Clark Rasmussen, toured the various district caucus meetings to promote the new state constitution and its endorsement provisions. During their visits, they discovered unexpectedly stiff opposition from those who agreed with Hughes's initial contentions: that endorsements would ultimately divide the party in heated convention battles and that they would block rising newcomers from obtaining party nominations.[75]

However, in this, his last appearance at a state convention as party chairman, Hawkins staged his most memorable and spectacular performance. Determined to make the party appear triumphant over Hughes, Hawkins delivered a stunning hammer-and-tongs speech. Flinging his coat aside and striding about the convention dais in his shirtsleeves as he thrashed his arms through the air, Hawkins told the delegates they were "wasting their time" supporting candidates who did not live up to the party platforms. He repeated his earlier argument, this time in more striking terms, that candidates were presently chosen in smoke-filled rooms, even by Hawkins himself, with the primary system intact:

> I have illegally used the Democratic party machinery in support of candidates whom I wanted.
>
> I have used my power illegally to get Congressman Neal Smith nominated and elected. In 1962 I used the state chairman's job, the party machinery and party money to get Harold Hughes nominated over his opponent.
>
> I am not embarrassed by this.... I have been a dictator but the next chairman may not be as benevolent as I am.[76]

A PARTY REBORN
— 116 —

The speech electrified the delegates. When Hughes chose not to appear before the convention, they approved the Hawkins constitution with its endorsement provisions intact by an unexpected two-to-one margin.[77] From all appearances, Hawkins had left his Democratic post a champion. His party, his causes, and even his favored candidates had shared victories under his tutelage. The future looked promising.

THE 1966 ELECTIONS demonstrated that the overwhelming Democratic victories of 1964 were deceptive. Following a long succession of Democratic defeats, 1964 vote totals had created the impression of Democratic strength, but a permanent party organization had yet to be built. Even Lex Hawkins's endorsement scheme proved futile in November 1966, failing to shore up the organizational foundation. Backed by Hawkins, E. B. Smith won the Democrats' first (and, incidentally, last) convention endorsement in his second race for the U.S. Senate, this time against incumbent Republican Jack Miller.[78] As if to mock the earlier dramatic convention efforts of Hawkins, Miller romped to a decisive victory over Smith, winning, for the first time in any Iowa election, all 99 of the state's counties.

Fate treated the rest of the Democratic ticket much the same as Republicans gained back virtually all they had lost in the 1964 landslide. With the threatening specter of a Goldwater candidacy now passed, a record number of off-year voters expressed their discontent with the policies of the Johnson Administration, and to a certain extent with Hughes's progressivism as well. The Republicans attacked government spending, called for anti-inflation policies, and demanded intrepid leadership in the Vietnam conflict. Five of the seven Republicans who had run for Congress would now join Senator Miller in Washington, D.C. And

DEMOCRATS REBORN

in the statehouse urban Democrats had retained their seats, but Republicans had made astounding gains everywhere else, capturing 90 of 124 seats. In the Senate the Democrats won only nine of the 32 positions at stake and hung on to their once hefty majority by only three votes.[79]

After the 1966 election, some people may have recalled the historical pattern of Iowa Democratic victories since the 19th Century. It seemed Democrats had been welcomed into the legislative halls only in those low moments when citizens had feared themselves or their country to be on the verge of disaster. And not unlike scavenger birds, the Democrats had lost their strength and numbers as the crises had eased.

But in the decade following the 1966 debacle, Iowa Democrats were unleashed from the cycles of the past, and party leaders moved to resolve their most fundamental dichotomy. Three notable exceptions to the Republican trends in 1966 underscored the two different approaches to Iowa Democratic politics.

Harold E. Hughes had continued his winning ways. He became the first Democratic governor in Iowa's history to be elected to three terms. Lacking an extensive grass-roots organization, and still conducting campaigns based on serious issues—though no issue had emerged in this election as spectacular as his earlier advocacy of liquor-by-the-drink—Hughes attracted a wide, bipartisan, personal following. But his following did not extend to many other members of his own party.

On the other hand, the victories of Congressman Neal Smith and Congressman John C. Culver pointed to the continuing need for precinct-by-precinct organizations if Democratic candidates other than Hughes were to be elected. Smith, of course, still reaped the fruits of the Polk County machine he had helped to establish in his own Fifth

A PARTY REBORN
— 118 —

District. Culver's re-election in the Second District indicated that such organizational techniques could be used successfully in other parts of the state as well. The Second District had been a marginal district throughout the 1950s. Before Culver first ran in 1964, most Second District elections had been determined by less than a 55% to 45% edge. Culver, a brilliant, explosive, and hard-driving man, began in that first election to transform his area into a solidly Democratic one. He used the organizational skills he had learned both from Polk County workers and from managing the 1962 U.S. Senate campaign of Edward M. Kennedy, a former Harvard football teammate. Since 1964, all Iowa Democrats in Congress, including Culver, had been unusually successful in securing federally funded projects for their home districts, and the national press had focused upon the Iowa congressional races as a "referendum" on the Johnson Administration policies. Alone of the freshman representatives, Culver survived the test, pointing to the strengths of both the candidate himself and his campaign organization. In that election, without a Johnson landslide to help him, Culver had increased his margin of victory.[80] In each successive election, Culver would expand that margin. And those victories would provide an inspirational and tactical example to party workers across the state, much as had the earliest surprising successes of the Polk County Democrats.

Yet in 1966 Smith and Culver were clearly exceptions in the congressional races. Developments would grow even worse for the Democrats; two years later, the Republicans would win nearly everything. In the years following, however, two fundamental processes would complete the transfiguration of the Iowa Democratic Party. First, Harold Hughes would continue to alter the very constituency of his own party as he openly and defiantly advocated new

DEMOCRATS REBORN
– 119 –

and unpopular stands on important political issues. And, second, behind him a new breed of rising politicians, faithful to the ideological tenets of Hughes, yet also true believers in the necessity for effective party organization, would emerge on the political forefront to usher the Democrats into a new political ascendancy.

During his third term as governor, Harold Hughes launched his party into a new phase of social activism, hammering away at conservative impediments to reform. In this, his final term, he convinced a divided legislature to reorganize the state's tax structure completely along more progressive lines and to remodel the government according to more rational schemes. Larry L. King summarized Hughes's accomplishments in *Harpers*:

> Harold Hughes managed effective prison reforms, established a State Law Enforcement Academy, reshaped the Highway Patrol along more gentle lines, and abolished capital punishment. He obtained Iowa's first alcoholic treatment facility and its first public defender; he tripled state aid to education and was aggressive in conserving parks and other public recreational works. His administration got an industrial-safety law and twice increased workmen's compensation benefits, pushed through a bill to control billboard advertising along state highways, and gave the state its first consumer-protection laws of any consequence. His fiscal reforms included repeal of the property tax on household goods and reduction of taxes for the elderly poor, an increase in state income tax, and a tax withholding system greatly aiding revenue collections which had in the past been hit or miss.[81]

In the meantime, Hughes expanded his role as spokesman for a changing Iowa electorate. Iowa voters in November had voiced a deep—if vaguely defined—disappointment with the Johnson Administration. Now they saw their governor, as chairman of the Democratic National Governors Conference, courageously confront the President at his Texas ranch, conveying the Conference's concern over Johnson's performance.

A PARTY REBORN

Hughes also squarely faced perhaps the most polarizing national political issue in the post-World War II era: racial discrimination.[82] Even though the state had less than a 1% minority population, Iowa citizens shared in the national alarm and confusion when racial disturbances broke out in other parts of the country. As the large slums of other northern cities burned, the governor himself walked through the quiet streets and into church basements of pocket ghettos in Des Moines and Waterloo to demonstrate his concern. He also established a Human Rights Commission and pushed for an open-housing law, while securing public and private means to aid the unemployed minorities.

It was on the issue of the Vietnam War, however, that Hughes best personified and symbolized the metamorphosis of moral and political attitudes in Iowa. Both the 1964 and 1966 state Democratic platforms had pledged support for the American war efforts. In his 1967 State of the State Message, Hughes himself had criticized war protesters when he described the "backlash" of "anti-warfare." "We seize upon some isolated incident to justify the prejudice we secretly carried in our hearts all the time," he proclaimed.[83] Earlier in 1967, he had openly expressed his affection for President Johnson, pledging his support for a President burdened by the responsibilities of war. "Mr. President, if you are going to be the horse, I don't mind being the bangle on the tail," Hughes told the President.[84]

But in 1968, after struggling with the Vietnam issue in a personal as well as public way, Hughes voiced his unequivocal opposition to the American war efforts when he delivered the nominating speech for Eugene McCarthy at the 1968 Democratic National Convention in Chicago. Upon his return to Iowa, Hughes entered the race for the United States Senate and became one of the few Senate candidates in the nation, of any political persuasion, to run a campaign based on opposition to Johnson's war policies.[85] "I don't care what it does to my campaign," he said, acknowledging that his war views smashed headlong against the majority of Iowa public opinion. "I'm interested in saving lives, not in politics. I just want to get the war over with."[86]

Hughes's outspokenness on these issues made the Democratic Party of Iowa, already the party of Harold E. Hughes, now also clearly the progressive party of Iowa. It occurred just as the American electorate re-aligned along new and increasingly ideological lines.[87] Alone among leaders of either party in Iowa, Hughes used powerful national symbols to alter the image of the state Democrats.

Hughes gained political strength by his ability to address the frustrations of many Iowa voters who felt unable to express themselves politically on burning national and state issues. He also sensed their disgruntlement with the organizational and institutional obstacles that the political system had placed in the way of free expression of their views. He took steps as well to achieve meaningful reform of the party structure. As a member of the "McGovern-Fraser Commission," Hughes pushed hard for changes in the national party structure. In Iowa, he convinced the 1970 state convention to pass important reforms: annual conventions (rather than just election year meetings) to be held at the county, district, and state level to discuss issues; members of the platform and resolution committees to be elected, rather than appointed by county chairmen as in the past; a minimum age for delegates of 18 rather than 21 years; all delegations to be proportionally representative of "men, women, age groups, racial minority groups and economic groups" of the districts from which they came; and all delegations to national conventions to be elected, not appointed, by the district and the state presidential conventions.[88]

A study of the 1968 and 1972 Democratic and Republican conventions in Iowa revealed that in those years of reform a whole new stratum of activists became involved in the Democratic Party convention politics while the Republican delegations remained relatively unchanged. By the 1972 convention, Democratic delegates were younger, less experienced in convention politics, and representative of a wider range of occupations than their Republican counterparts. Two Iowa political scientists noted: "the number of pre-1955 Democrats dropped precipitously between the 1968 and 1972 conventions. The total effect indicates that these years—1968-1972—did occasion a considerable turnover of activists within the Democratic Party, replacing especially those who had been active in the period before 1955. The Republican Party by comparison shows a much more enduring activist membership."[89]

The decline of Harold E. Hughes's popularity as he conducted his campaign for the Senate against Muscatine's moderate Republican David Stanley further indicated the vascillating political loyalties in the state. Stanley attacked Hughes's strongest asset, the Governor's image as a politician of candor and integrity. Stanley charged that Hughes had changed his position on such issues as gun control, right-to-work laws, and the war itself.[90] Backed by enormous financial contributions from his own wealthy family, Stanley grasped at the domestic and foreign policy coattails of Richard Nixon with a billboard campaign that stated: "Nixon Needs Stanley." On a brick wall in Cedar Rapids that carried the Stanley slogan, a citizen replied in white letters, unevenly painted, "America Needs Hughes," and Hughes raised his own billboards proclaiming: "New Strength for Iowa." As Hughes stumped the state, he

DEMOCRATS REBORN
— 123 —

argued that his own record demonstrated a pattern of continuity, not sway.[91] Then, labelling the Vietnam War the "Johnson-Stanley War," Hughes relied upon his evangelical style to rally Iowans against the Southeast Asian military incursions, as *Des Moines Register* reporter James Flansburg recorded:

> On the campaign trail, Hughes builds toward his position by a profound plea for peace, then a description of the horrors of nuclear, germ and gas warfare that usually leaves his audiences silent.
> He lets the silence become loud, then repeats his first point: "Peace on earth. Good will toward men. The message that comes from every church edifice in this country. By every great religion known to mankind. And yet we have become so oriented to war and the building of destructive machinery that there are few who raise their voice and question how long we can continue in this capacity. How long must we build toward destruction? I raise this question in America and in Iowa!"[92]

On election day, Hughes barely escaped defeat. The same man who four years earlier had won by 429,479 votes, now won by only a 6,415-vote edge.[93] In the rest of the races, Iowa Democrats suffered devastating losses. Behind the strong lead of Richard M. Nixon (who, in Iowa, received about 53% of the vote to Hubert Humphrey's 41% and George Wallace's 6%) the Republicans won control of both chambers of the General Assembly, and Robert D. Ray easily defeated former Democratic State Treasurer Paul Franzenburg for the governorship. All seven incumbent congressmen won in their bids for re-election. Five of them were Republicans. Neal Smith and John Culver remained the only Iowa Democrats in the House. In all, the 1968 election exposed most nakedly what had first been revealed two years earlier. Hughes, an immensely popular politician, had a personal following loyal enough to secure statewide election victories for himself, even if he embraced unpopular and strongly articulated views. But his personal popularity did not immediately transfer to other Democrats. The only other successful Democratic candidates were those who combined their own localized popularity with dynamic district organizations.

NEW REPUBLICAN GOVERNOR ROBERT D. RAY combined youthful good looks with an iron will and an unusually even-keeled personality. A vivid episode during Ray's 1968 primary campaign had clearly demonstrated Ray's temperament to Iowans. Flying in a chartered plane near Mason City enroute to a political meeting, Ray barely escaped death when the aircraft plunged to the ground. The impact of the crash had broken Ray's leg, but the pilot later reported Ray's last words before the candidate had lost consciousness. "I hate to be a back-seat driver," Ray had told the pilot, "but I just saw some telephone poles go past the window."[94]

Once in office, Ray fought his harshest battles with conservative members of his own party as he sought ways to finance and streamline the social programs designed and legislated in the Hughes years. Yet Ray's style of leadership stood in clear contrast to that of Hughes. Quiet in his assertiveness, Ray most often labelled himself a "political pragmatist," refraining from moralism in the political arena. Nor did the new governor seek to involve himself in national issues not directly affecting Iowa.

It is unlikely Ray attracted the same constituency as Hughes, but he demonstrated that a progressive Republican, as well as a Democrat, could build a political coalition appealing to liberal urban areas.[95] In fact, Ray so completely captured the progressive constituency of the state that several Democratic challengers were now forced to present a more conservative image to voters in order to glean anti-Ray support. In 1970, Robert Fulton, architect

DEMOCRATS REBORN

of many of the programs legislated in the Hughes years, ran against Ray in the closest gubernatorial contest in 16 years, but he found himself robbed of the very issues he had once brought to the political forefront. As he explains:

> Ray closed in on us in so many areas, I couldn't draw distinctive lines to differentiate us—and that is the responsibility of the challenger. Straight down the line, Ray had taken stands on the issues that I had fought for during all twelve years of my political career. So that left me with one issue: taxes. The agricultural prices were going down, and I knew this meant that the tax receipts would also fall. I attacked Ray on this issue and called for raises in the statewide progressive taxes. In calling for the raises in the taxes, I lost the support of the urban vote, because they tend to look at property taxes as business costs, and they were overburdened by the large taxes.[96]

Given the remarkable success of Robert Ray and his ability to blur the ideological lines once drawn so distinctly by Harold Hughes, one might have expected Iowa Democrats to recoil into their historically conditioned posture of defeat, just as they had done in the late 1930s after a brief period of success. With Hughes now in Washington and concerned primarily with national problems, state Democrats were without the one personality around which much of the party's image in the 1960s had been formed.

But the Democratic Party did not collapse. Instead, a new generation of Democratic leaders came to the fore to make the solid state-wide organizational changes necessary to preserve it and, then, to increase those gains Hughes had earlier made in a personal way. The restructuring of the party organization (perhaps the most important reason for new Democratic gains in the 1970s) became possible when the enthusiasm and energies of the party's younger, more progressive membership combined with the traditional sources of organizational power, such as labor,[97] to build cooperatively a strong and rejuvenated party.

Representative John C. Culver and aide Richard C. Clark, 1970
COURTESY JOHN C. CULVER

V

THE ORGANIZED DEMOCRATS: JOHN CULVER, DICK CLARK AND THE NEW PARTY MACHINERY

IN JANUARY 1975 AT THE STATE CAPITOL in Des Moines, Republican Robert D. Ray prepared for his unprecedented fourth consecutive term as Iowa's governor. Though his personal electoral success was constant, Ray governed a state whose political complexion had been dramatically changed by the 1974 elections. He found the state legislature, which had become the most equitably apportioned legislature in the nation, now controlled by Democrats who were younger, more urban, and more diverse occupationally than members of previous General Assemblies.[1] In the State Senate, the Democrats enjoyed a slim majority. Across the rotunda, with a margin of 62-38, representatives expected to elect a Democrat speaker of the House, historically a position rarely held by members of that party. And in the 99 county courthouses where citizens are most apt to deal directly with their elected officials, Democrats now occupied a majority of Iowa's county offices for the first time since before the Civil War.

Also in the 1974 elections, Iowa Democratic candidates for national offices had shown greater strength than in previous years. John C. Culver, a ten-year veteran congressman from the Second District, led the ticket. He clipped Republican challenger David M. Stanley of Musca-

A PARTY REBORN

tine in their contest for the United States Senate seat left vacant by Harold Hughes's retirement from politics. Five of six Democrats running for congressional seats joined Culver in victory. Though public reaction to the Nixon Administration and the Watergate scandals may have explained some Democratic gains, the increased strength of the Democratic Party organization itself served as a foundation for many of the victories. By invigorating their party in the early 1970s, Iowa Democrats contradicted one of the most notable trends of the time, the disintegration of political parties. Party vitality in the United States had been declining since World War II as reform movements drained them of their traditional influences. Parties lost their ability to reward jobs to loyalists when civil service reforms cut the lines of patronage that in earlier eras had linked the administrative personnel of government to the outcome of campaigns and elections. Political parties ceased to be the principal sources of funding to candidates for public offices when private political groups and action committees, public subsidies, and sophisticated direct mail operations increasingly provided campaign financing. Finally, parties no longer controlled the gateways to the elective offices themselves because primary elections had superceded party nominating caucuses and conventions. The traditional organizations were left with little function other than to offer platforms to the candidates who shared their party label, planks the candidates, in turn, might embrace or eschew without praise or blame.

    Accompanying this national trend of political party decay was the tendency for more voters to register as Independents and "split" their tickets. Thus, people voted for candidates of two or even more political parties. By 1974, only one-fourth of the American electorate strongly identi-

ORGANIZED DEMOCRATS
— 129 —

fied with a political party, and, of those partisans who voted in the 1974 elections, more than one-half abandoned their party at least once to vote for a candidate of a different political persuasion.[2]

In Iowa, this development had serious implications for the way Democrats identified voters. The new voter volatility required from the party an increased sensitivity to the changing sentiments of the public. When Lex Hawkins started his voter-identification efforts in the early 1950s, he had gained his most crucial information by simply asking persons in selected urban areas about their party allegiances. Now, 20 years later, voters were much more apt to remain undecided on any particular race until close to election. To cope with the 1970s voters' fleeting partisan loyalties and growing attachments to personalities and issues, Democratic candidates promoted their own personalities and their personal positions on specific issues. As close to election as possible, party workers contacted all Iowa voters. They identified voters according to their general *party leaning* and, more importantly, according to their expressed *candidate preferences.* Using this information, Democrats then aimed special propaganda mailings at those voters they identified as still undecided about particular races. In addition, they targeted those voters favoring Democrats more than Republicans for voter-registration and election-day efforts. These new methods of identifying transitory voter allegiances required sophisticated new technologies and expanded financial support. The party replaced the shoestring budgets and shoebox filing systems of the earliest Polk County efforts with enormous capital outlays and computer memories. Indeed, in 1973 and 1974 alone, Democrats would spend $400,000 on their Voter Identification Program and other election day plans.[3]

A PARTY REBORN

Iowa Democratic politics in the 1960s and 1970s became notable for the ways it both paralleled and deviated from the flow of America's political currents. The tendency of voters to break their allegiances to political parties, replacing them with ties to personalities and issues, accelerated in Iowa just as it did throughout the nation. But Iowa Democrats increased their organizational capacities in this same time period, pointing the state's political practices in a direction that differed from the national trends.

That Iowa Democrats could construct such a program in the 1970s for the entire state was a result of events, trials, and errors of nearly a decade, and, particularly, of three essential developments. First, Democrats battled the Republican efforts to make voter registration more difficult in urban counties, eventually passing new legislation that made voting requirements uniform and registration more easily accessible to all Iowans. Second, Democratic leaders established new means to make the state party organization solvent and economically capable of supporting statewide campaign and identification efforts. Finally, Democratic activists and candidates backed a centralized party strategy that sometimes pre-empted their own campaign plans.

Ever since voter registration statutes had frustrated Polk County Democrats in the 1950s, party members sought to remedy the situation through revision of Iowa's election laws. Between 1969 and 1973, Democrats gradually eased the burden of registration responsibilities. In the 1965 General Assembly, the Democratic majority changed the state's laws to dictate modifications of registration requirements such as those tried in Des Moines in all of the state's registration cities (those with populations of more than 10,000). In particular, the law allowed the establishment of branch registration sites in those cities during the first week

ORGANIZED DEMOCRATS

of October, aiding the registration efforts of urban organizations and labor unions.[4] Members of the Republican-controlled 1970 General Assembly seemed determined to increase the difficulties of voter registration efforts by the Democrats, for they imposed a new stipulation: now all residents of counties with more than 50,000 residents (not just the larger cities of those counties) had to be registered to vote. There was no apparent reason for the bill other than that the 100,000 citizens directly affected by this law were not likely to vote for candidates of the GOP. Now about one-half of Iowa's voters were required to register, and most of this group lived in Democratic strongholds.[5] The discriminatory nature of the statute prompted Democrats in the 1974 General Assembly to rewrite the provisions completely. Thereafter, *all* voters in the state were required to register but they could do so via postcard, mobile registrar, or in person at various public institutions. No longer did Iowa voting laws place the Democratic Party at a competitive disadvantage with the rival Republicans.

Efforts to provide the state Democratic Party with a sound fiscal foundation proved considerably more difficult. From 1966 to 1972, the party's attempts to assume additional responsibilities had frequently been frustrated by a lack of funds. In 1966, for example, party members, under the guidance of State Chairman Clark Rasmussen, attempted to raise money systematically for the first time. They collected nearly $300,000 but found themselves $150,000 in debt after electon day and $40,000 behind a year later.[6] By 1971, the party still owed over $70,000 that Rasmussen's successor, Cliff Larson, could not pay, even though the organization raised over $140,000 that year.[7]

With some irony, the state's Republicans, reacting to the scandals of Watergate, finally enabled the Democratic

Party to become solvent. For several years Democrats had sought to pass a state income tax check-off law resembling the national program. Citizens could choose, by checking a box on their tax forms, to pay one tax dollar to support one party or the other in lieu of paying the dollar to the state treasury. Their attempts had been unsuccessful until Iowa Republicans in the 1973 legislature, now more anxious to improve the methods of financing political parties and election campaigns, finally agreed to the check-off bill of the Democrats.[8]

The national check-off law and check-off statutes written in other states channeled money directly to individual candidates. By contrast, the Iowa bill was designed to funnel the funds through, and thereby to increase the power of, the state party organization. The authors of the bill, staff members of the state Democratic Party, intended the state party to conduct voter-identification and voter-registration programs on behalf of the candidates themselves. Beginning in 1973, the Democratic Party received at least $120,000 per year from the tax check-off, out-distancing the Republican Party by about a three-to-two margin. With these funds, the Democrats managed to pull themselves out of debt and to finance effective campaign activities.[9]

As the Democrats acquired the financial capacity to support statewide programs, the party received additional and critical boosts from energetic politicians eager for statewide offices. John C. Culver and Dick Clark invested their own resources to strengthen the organization. Unlike the Iowa Democrats, politicians of other states, in their own cities, counties, or congressional districts, often established personal fiefdoms; in those states, politicians sought little help from, and offered little support to, central state party administrations. In Iowa, on the other hand, Culver

ORGANIZED DEMOCRATS

and Clark shared their own tried and tested designs, developed earlier in Culver's Second District congressional races, with the entire state party and for a very good reason. They themselves were soon running for United States Senate seats.

More than any other Iowa Democrat, Congressman Culver had transformed the momentum of the 1964 Democratic landslide into the detailed work necessary to create a secure political base. When other Iowa Democratic congressmen had subsequently been swept out of office, only Culver increased his margin of victory in each of four more elections. Of course, Culver's campaigning and legislating style played a crucial role in his growing popularity. But his organizational plans translated his popularity into broadening majority votes on election days. Culver's assistant, Dick Clark, orchestrated the campaigns, assembling teams of volunteers to identify and list potential Democratic voters, registering likely supporters at the county courthouses, and mounting massive election-day drives.

Clark and Culver demonstrated the power and the benefits of organization when Iowans elected both of them to the Senate. When Culver first eyed the 1972 Senate election and the seat held by two-term incumbent Republican Jack Miller, he and Clark pushed the state party to organize all of Iowa after the pattern of the Second District operation. In February 1972, Culver stunned the state by deciding not to run after all. Clark followed with a surprise of his own, entering the race for the Senate on his own behalf and continuing to use a less ambitious version of the planned Culver-Clark attack. The results startled Iowans and the nation. Clark overwhelmed Senator Miller, and even Senator George McGovern showed unanticipated strength in Iowa in his losing battle against Richard M. Nixon for the presidency.

A PARTY REBORN

Issues and personalities both played prominent roles in the Clark and McGovern showings. In the aftermath, however, the party revitalized its commitment to strengthening its organizational muscle. Harold Hughes initiated plans to establish a statewide machinery for his own anticipated 1974 re-election bid to the U.S. Senate, based on Clark's earlier model. But he cancelled his personal 1973 re-election campaign, and Culver immediately charged into the race as Hughes's replacement. With the enthusiastic support of the party, Culver picked up where Hughes had left off, expanded the parameters of the 1972 organization and further refined its methods. In January 1975, Culver took the oath of office to become Iowa's second Democratic senator.

The Clark and Culver Senate candidacies, and their shared desire to build this statewide political machinery in the wake of Harold Hughes, served to distinguish Iowa's politics in the 1970s from the national picture. Despite the public's growing cynicism about government and despite widespread political party decay, the unprecedented Democratic gains in 1974 were no accident of history, nor were they an unavoidable reaction to Watergate. Rather, the advances resulted from the workings of a new party machinery which consolidated rational long-term planning, adequate funding, additional paid staff workers, and, above all, the efforts of thousands of volunteers.

Bold and forceful leadership, backed by new political technology, worked in Iowa, and worked well. Democratic politicians became less inclined to conduct their personal campaigns alone, detached from the party machinery. Widespread Democratic victories had occurred when that machinery reached its peak of strength in 1974. Even though the organization was at its zenith in 1974, its parts had been created, studied and refined for nearly ten years in the Second Congressional District.

ORGANIZED DEMOCRATS
— 135 —

IN THE YEARS IMMEDIATELY FOLLOWING WORLD WAR II, Republicans continued politically to dominate the Second District. Tucked away in Iowa's northeast corner, far from the site of Polk County's Democratic revival in the 1950s, the Second District had seldom seen an interruption in Republican control for more than a century. According to the reapportionment following the 1940 Census, twelve counties comprised the district—Allamakee, Benton, Buchanan, Clayton, Clinton, Delaware, Dubuque, Fayette, Jackson, Jones, Linn, and Winneshiek (a subsequent reapportionment put Benton County in the First District). Bordered on the east by the Mississippi River and on the north by Minnesota, citizens here had become accustomed to a quiet style of politics, developed amid the traditional rhythms of life first established by their rural German and Scandinavian ancestors. Rolling hills nestled the bountiful soils, and the hard-working, ruggedly individualistic farm families prospered. Together, the district's counties ranked in the top ten of all the nation's 435 congressional districts in the value of their agricultural production. The economy of the Second District enjoyed a fortunate balance. North of Highway 20, on the district's more rugged terrain, farmers produced the bulk of Iowa's dairy goods. Their farms were among the smallest in the state. South of the highway, on larger farms with richer soil, farmers specialized in breeding cattle and raising corn. The cities in the southern sector hosted Iowa's major corn and oat milling businesses and shipped rural grains to urban processing centers. Many of Iowa's colleges and universities as well as highly sophisticated technological industries, such as Collins Radio Company in Cedar Rapids, were also located in the district. In this part of the state, the labors of the hand were balanced by the labors of the mind.

A PARTY REBORN

As throughout Iowa in the postwar years, important changes in the Second District's economy anticipated a transition in its political climate. By the 1950s over one-half of the district's population had shifted from rural to urban areas (that is, communities with a population exceeding 2,500 persons). Of the approximately 400,000 residents then living in its counties, nearly three-fourths of the urban population (155,000 persons) lived in three fast-growing manufacturing cities: Cedar Rapids, Dubuque, and Clinton. As sites for industries making both agricultural and technological goods, these larger cities developed important national and international exporting markets and a cosmopolitan outlook which stood, at times, in vivid contrast to the traditional views of the district's rural and agrarian past. New attitudes and new governmental needs tugged at the political fabric woven over a century.

At first, few Democratic Party advances in the postwar era accompanied the important and accelerated economic changes. From 1941 until 1963, not one Democrat was elected to any county office in Allamakee, Benton, and Fayette counties. In fact, no Democrat had won a county office in Allamakee County since 1936. Although active Democratic minorities existed in Clinton and Linn counties, only in Dubuque County did there exist a traditional Democratic reservoir. One man had represented the district in Washington, D.C. during this time of rapid economic transition, Republican Congressman Henry O. Talle of Decorah. Reserved and dignified, an economics professor by trade, interpreting his role in Congress to be more a "legislator" than a "public figure," Talle had offered northeast Iowa a passive—and popular—style of politics and campaigning since 1938.[10] Returning to the state for an occasional recess, Talle kept a relatively low profile at home and hustled back to his perch in Washington,

ORGANIZED DEMOCRATS
— 137 —

D.C. to monitor legislation. Not often supporting an expanded role for the federal government beyond the limits established by the New Deal, Talle had seemed determined to protect Iowans from new federal programs rather than trying to activate citizen participation with federal agencies. In the 1958 elections, when Iowa farmers expressed their rage at the low market prices caused by the Eisenhower Administration farm policies, Republican Talle suffered defeat along with four of his Iowa GOP congressional colleagues.

Democrat Leonard G. Wolf of Elkader, the winner of the 1958 contest, managed to hold the seat for only one term. But in that short span, he established a new *modus operandi* for the Second District congressmen who followed him, a new activism stressing constituent service and a higher degree of local visibility. Wolf acquired a trailer, painted it brightly, staffed it with paid assistants, drove it around the district, parked it in conspicuous places, and administered to the needs of constituents. As a former feed-grain dealer in Elkader, Wolf quickly established an easy rapport with the area's rural residents. Indeed, in only one term Wolf transformed the role of congressman in the Second District from that of a distant "legislator" to that of a mingling, accessible, even dynamic representative, attentive to the immediate needs of his constituents.[11]

Iowa's 1960 Republican landslide ended the congressional career of Leonard G. Wolf. Republican attorney James R. Bromwell of Cedar Rapids won the seat back for his party. Following the pattern established by Wolf, Congressman Bromwell worked hard to become visible in the communities of the district, averaging one trip to the state every ten days. Bromwell's activist nature led him to make as many as five speeches in one day, ninety speeches in one three-month span. He experimented with polling tech-

A PARTY REBORN

niques to gauge public opinion in the district and to supplement the informal questions he asked during his frequent personal appearances. Bromwell also used newsletters and television shows to promote his ideas to his constituents, being perhaps the first Iowa congressman to use television for that purpose.[12]

If Bromwell's style pointed to the future, his rhetoric and politics pointed more to the district's past. In wrestling the congressional seat from Leonard G. Wolf, Bromwell had centered his most frequent attacks upon the expanded role of the federal government. "I was an unembarrassed conservative," remembered Bromwell later.[13] Indeed, in many ways his 1960 victory, and his re-election in 1962, suggested the Second District of Iowa had returned to a slightly altered form of its earlier political "normalcy," reminiscent of times before the Democrat Wolf had interrupted the flow of events. With a Republican incumbent who was not only ambitious and highly visible, but who also professed political values echoing the long-standing views of Henry O. Talle, few saw omens of the imminent rise of the Democratic Party in the Second District.

However, in the fall of 1963 Democrat John C. Culver and his wife Ann returned to their Linn County home. Culver tacked his shingle to the door of a local firm in Cedar Rapids and announced his intention to practice law. Immediately there was speculation about his possible candidacy for political office, perhaps for the congressional seat held by James Bromwell. Culver's reappearance created a stir in Cedar Rapids partly because he had previously talked of his interests in Iowa politics and, particularly, because of his ties to the national political drama of "Camelot."

When John Culver had followed in the footsteps of his father and grandfather in 1950 to attend Harvard College,

ORGANIZED DEMOCRATS

he had taken with him an avid interest in sports and politics. Selected in Cedar Rapids for all-city and all-state honorable mention in football at Franklin High School, Culver was recruited by both Coach Dr. Eddie Anderson of the University of Iowa and by the coaching staff of Harvard College. Culver chose Harvard and captured Eastcoast and Iowa headlines when he set single-season and single-game scoring records for the Crimson, collecting academic all-America honors along the way. At fullback and defensive team player, Culver acquired a reputation for his fiercely competitive spirit and his unbending desire to win. With his famous touchdown run against Yale in 1953 (captured on film by a Boston *Globe* photographer and wired across the nation), Culver etched his moment into the annals of Harvard sports history. In his senior year, Culver was drafted by the (then) Chicago Cardinals and, after graduating from college, he considered a possible career in professional football.

But Culver never played in a professional game. Instead, he decided to pursue his interests in government and politics. The son of prominent Republican parents, Culver had demonstrated his earliest inclination for elective office during high school. In 1949, he had been elected secretary of state at the American Legion Boys' State Convention at Camp Dodge.

Culver's studies at Harvard furthered his interests in government and politics. He wrote his honors thesis on the reapportionment issue in Iowa. "I actually went pretty much through college with political attitudes which were consistent with those I was most familiar with in my home," Culver later recalled. "As I became further interested, had increased studies, and enjoyed the opportunity to travel, I found my personal attitudes more sympathetic to the general programs and principles of the Democratic

A PARTY REBORN

Party."[14] Culver's development as a progressive Democrat did not occur overnight, and it did not occur automatically, but was the result of experiences in his post-graduate years before returning to Iowa.

After graduation, Culver was awarded Harvard College's prestigious Lionel de Jersey scholarship, and, declining the offer to play professional football, he left for England. There at Cambridge's Emmanuel College, living in the same room where three centuries earlier John Harvard had studied before sailing to Massachusetts, Culver continued his study of politics and government. Beginning to stray from the political views inherited from his immediate family, Culver travelled across Europe that year and then returned to the United States in 1955 to enlist in the Marine Corps.[15]

As a Marine, Culver rose to the rank of infantry officer, developing strategic skills that would one day leave their mark on his style of political campaigning. Restless, bored with the administrative duties assigned to him as infantry officer, Culver asked to be reassigned to field duties. His request was granted, and he was sent to the Philippine Islands where he excelled in training missions and war-game exercises. Cast as the leader of "enemy" forces, Culver swung into action, barking orders to his strike troops, and exhibiting skills in strategy which later would be directed towards politics. Culver switched from his inherited Republicanism to the Democrats during his time at Harvard Law School. In 1962, amid his student activities and studies, Culver renewed his undergraduate friendship with football teammate Edward M. Kennedy, who was then launching his campaign for the United States Senate. Culver played a key role in Kennedy's campaign. Just as Kennedy's older brothers had made indispensable political aides of some of their former football teammates, he made

ORGANIZED DEMOCRATS

Culver a chief strategist and advisor in this, his first successful Senate campaign.[16]

Following Kennedy's victory, Culver, with his wife and three children, moved to Washington where he served as the senator's legislative assistant. Working with Kennedy whetted Culver's own political appetite for elective office, and he returned to Cedar Rapids in September 1963 to begin immediate testing of the political waters in the Second District. The speculation surrounding his reappearance was well-informed. Culver readied to oppose Republican incumbent James Bromwell for the congressional seat in the next election.

Three qualities marked Culver's initial Second District campaign that would also characterize all his subsequent campaigns. First, Culver's political style incorporated elements from his academic football, Marine Corps, and Kennedy-campaign experiences. A thoroughly prepared, highly visible, and hard-hitting approach became the hallmark of Culver's bids for office. Second, Culver used issues effectively, combining his own beliefs with a rising progressive mood in the Second District, in his pursuit of votes. Except during Leonard G. Wolf's brief, earlier appearance, many of these progressive instincts had not been clearly expressed in Second District politics. Culver now became their spokesman. Finally, and importantly, Culver and his assistant Dick Clark developed a campaign organization strong enough, when associated with Culver's style and beliefs, to broaden his political base, identify his political following, and draw out the maximum number of votes in a district traditionally considered a Republican stronghold.

In depth and sophistication, Culver's first campaign had no precedent in Iowa politics. The political machinery developed under his and Clark's direction, supported by

A PARTY REBORN

the work of hundreds of volunteers, later pulled Culver majorities to the polls even when other Democratic congressmen found themselves overwhelmed by fast-changing public sentiment.

Culver's aggressive approach to campaigning became evident in that initial bid for office when he moved to prevent his strongest potential Democratic rival from entering into the primary race. Prior to Culver's return to the District, in the congressional election of 1962, incumbent Repubican James Bromwell had been stiffly challenged by Democrat Frank Less, a native of Cascade who practiced law and managed farms. A lifelong Democrat from a farming community, Less reminded campaign audiences of his background as a farmer, as well as his urban ties, and he attracted a strong following. Until the arrival of Culver, most people had assumed that Less would be the automatic Democratic candidate for Congress again in 1964, should he decide to run again.

Culver worked to block a Less comeback. Practicing law by day in Cedar Rapids, after work and on weekends Culver drove thousands of miles throughout the district to establish his own ties with party activists in every county. Starting with a modest list of people active in John F. Kennedy's 1960 presidential campaign, Culver spent the early months building support in the parlors of private homes and booths of small-town cafes. Arriving at the cafes in late afternoon, his pocket full of dimes, Culver called his list of local activists and invited them to talk about politics, often soliciting their support for his planned candidacy and asking for names of other potential local supporters.[17]

In the beginning, Culver relied upon the volunteer assistance of two key people. Teri Ferguson, a former League of Women Voters activist from Linn County, now waited in Cedar Rapids for Culver to return from the far corners of the district so she could fire off letters to the people Culver had seen, encouraging their future support. Starting a file of index cards, she established a catalogue of everyone with whom Culver had met, listing the dates, locations, and reasons for each encounter. She also attached pertinent personal information which might be useful later in the campaign. She dutifully recorded any births, deaths, or marriages Culver might someday wish to acknowledge.[18]

Richard C. Clark, 35, a history instructor at Upper Iowa University in Fayette, Iowa, served Culver as his most vital assistant in the first campaign and subsequently in the first four terms of Culver's congressional career. In 1962, as Democratic chairman of Fayette precinct, which encompassed the entire city of Fayette, Clark had experimented with canvassing and election day activities. Told of the gains made by Lex Hawkins and the Polk County Democrats, Clark used students to canvass every household in the area to assess the political inclinations of each of the city's voters. Filing index cards in shoe boxes in the Polk County tradition, Clark and his students sorted the data by political preference. Then, taking the boxes of "Independent" cards with him, Clark spent an evening with the elderly postmaster of Fayette, a Democrat appointed during the Roosevelt Administration. Together they estimated the political leanings of each "Independent." By election day, Clark had generated an effective strategy to increase the number of Democratic votes in a precinct that had not *once* in its history voted for a statewide Democratic candidate:

We opened a storefront office in downtown Fayette which I had rented for two days for $20. There, we got on the phones on election day and kept calling all day long the people we thought would vote for the Democrats. We had poll watchers with matching lists. The Republicans of course, having won all previous gubernatorial elections, including

1960, had the majority of poll watchers, and they were surprised to see Democrats watching the polls, too.

By early evening all but 30 to 40 of our people had voted. So we started calling their friends and neighbors to give them encouragement. In the end, all but one or two of our people had voted. Although a Democrat had never won in Fayette before, Harold Hughes won by a couple of votes.[19]

His surprising success brought Clark added notice in Demcratic circles. In 1963, he helped to organize opposition to the Shaff reapportionment plan. Having earlier won national recognition as a collegiate debater, Clark now used his oratorical and his political skills throughout eastern Iowa, contributing to the defeat of the Shaff Plan in December 1963. With these two experiences behind him, Clark offered valuable knowledge and an intuitive understanding of how to mount election-day drives and how to organize issues and people effectively, talents useful to any congressional campaign.[20]

J. D. Weimer, the Linn County Democratic Central Committee chairman, brought Clark's accomplishments to John Culver's attention. In October 1963, Culver went to Fayette to meet Clark. Culver describes their first encounter: "I knocked on his door and was very impressed with him and liked him right away. He was very well organized and had files of people, listed by county, who had been active in different causes such as civil rights. Dick had a natural organizational inclination that could be helpful, and soon we were working closer. In mid-December we decided he would be the campaign manager starting in January."[21]

With the logistical support supplied by Clark, Culver's congressional campaign became what the *Des Moines Register* later called perhaps "the most intensively organized congressional drive" theretofore witnessed in Iowa history.[22] Culver describes the campaign:

ORGANIZED DEMOCRATS

Dick and I, for the first time in the district, applied serious, rational study of voting patterns in the area and canvassed the precincts according to those studies, and with Dick's help, we applied some of the same strategies to my campaign: we aggressively used yard signs, bumper stickers; held fundraisers, coffees; and sent out mailings. We were, I think, the first campaign in the state to utilize the arsenal of campaign techniques — we tried to make them work, and we developed a serious volunteer effort.[23]

After Culver and Clark had analyzed congressional district voting patterns precinct-by-precinct, they created a priority ranking list of those precincts according to their estimated Culver-vote potential. Almost all 337 Second District precincts were assigned "Culver coordinators" to carry out campaign tasks. Culver himself covered the district by car and on foot. He pushed himself and his volunteers through 18-hour days. He shook enough hands to form a callus an inch-and-one-half long on his right palm. He chatted over tea and coffee with women's groups. And he pounded his fists on the podiums of labor halls.[24]

Confronted with Culver's ambition, Frank Less decided not to seek the Democratic congressional nomination. However, Dr. James E. Feld, a 31-year-old dentist from Oelwein and a close friend of Less, unexpectedly challenged Culver, chastising him for "forcing Less out of the race" and labelling Culver a "Kennedy plant."[25] The contest quickened the pulse of the Culver organization. He beat Feld in the June primary election by a margin of 11,197 to 6,673. Shortly after the defeat, an embittered Feld declared his support for the Republican incumbent James Bromwell.[26]

One of Culver's most difficult tasks was to become well-known in the congressional district in a short period of time. Even two-term incumbent Republican Bromwell, after two conspicuous campaigns, with a relatively dy-

A PARTY REBORN
— 146 —

namic congressional style, was still not well-known in the eleven-county area. In early 1964, a public opinion survey revealed less than 20% of the Second District voters could name Bromwell as their congressman. Becoming personally recognized by and familiar with the constituents carried an added burden for Culver. Many people in the Second District, especially those living north of Highway 20, still clung to prejudices against the Democratic Party apparently stretching back to the Civil War.

Culver confronted those prejudices face-to-face during a campaign swing through the northern tier of Second District counties. He later recalled:

> In Waukon, in Allamakee County, I was going door to door and I came upon three old farmers sitting on a park bench and I decided to approach and introduce myself to them. I shook hands with the first one and said:
>
> "I'm John Culver and I'm running for Congress."
>
> I did the same with the second, but neither seemed too interested. Just as I was reaching for the third man's hand, the first one interrupted:
>
> "Just a minute, young fella, what did you say you're running for?"
>
> "Congressman."
>
> "Tell me, are you a Republican or are you one of those Democrats?"
>
> "Why, sir," I told all three of them, "I'm a Democrat."
>
> The old timer shook his head, turned to his buddies and he told them:
>
> "You know, it's getting so when you scrub 'em up real good you can't tell a Democrat from a Republican any more."[27]

In the more populous areas, particularly in Cedar Rapids, Dubuque, and Clinton, Culver and Clark made special efforts to increase the candidate's visibility. They organized teams of volunteers—many of them from area schools and colleges, others from labor unions, and still more from the rank-and-file of party regulars. Culver and Clark sent the teams to the most heavily Democratic precincts to place

ORGANIZED DEMOCRATS

bumper stickers on cars, to gather voter registration and party preference information in door-to-door canvasses, and to place Culver yard signs on front lawns. Other volunteers, armed with campaign literature, joined Culver at factory gates as he greeted workers who entered and exited in the early morning hours.

Culver supplemented these sweeps through crucial areas with the less conspicuous preparations for election day conducted at campaign headquarters on First Avenue in Cedar Rapids, across the street from the Roosevelt Hotel. There Culver established banks of telephones where sat rows of volunteers calling the homes in priority precincts in Clinton, Dubuque, Cedar Rapids, and Oelwein to gain party preference information. Late into the evening, Culver headquarters bulged with supporters stuffing envelopes with his pamphlets and letters. Culver and Clark aimed each mailing at specific groups in the district, and printed them on campaign stationery announcing, "Leadership for the New Iowa."[28]

This first campaign organization and the ones which grew out of it, "played a central role" in Culver's congressional victories, maintained Dick Clark.[29] At the start of the 1964 campaign, Clark visited Lex Hawkins and Art Hedberg in Des Moines to discuss details of the Polk County Democratic practices. Based on those talks, his own instincts, and the methods Culver had learned in Edward Kennedy's 1962 Senate campaign, Clark fashioned an election day strategy to maximize Democratic votes. The Republicans planned for election day in their usual modest way, noting the names of Republicans who had voted in the course of the day and calling those who had not come to the polls. By contrast, Culver and Clark readied to pull and coax to the voting booths all Democrats and sympathetic Independents they were able to identify in advance

A PARTY REBORN

through the extensive telephone and limited door-to-door canvasses. Each Culver volunteer in Cedar Rapids, Clinton, Dubuque, and Oelwein was assigned to work a particular precinct. On election day, in the Polk County tradition, Clark and Culver gave each volunteer a list of about 100 previously identified voters, arranged in walking order. With lists in hand, the volunteers and other team members visited each designated voter who had not yet gone to the polls and encouraged each to vote. By nightfall they offered the non-voters baby sitters, rides, and campaign literature which advised a Culver vote.[30]

The thoroughness of the Culver organization marked the real beginning of a new era in Iowa politics, a beginning foreshadowed years earlier in Polk County. When Leonard G. Wolf and Frank Less ran for Congress in the Second District, their small circles of assistants relied almost exclusively on the existing Democratic Party for money and aid in campaigning. The essential funding for both had come from the various county central committees. However, without depending on the party, Culver raised well over $50,000 for his own campaign treasury and established an operation whose basic loyalty was to his own candidacy.[31] County central committees and party regulars played an important role in the various Culver campaign activities—many of the 337 precinct Culver coordinators were also central committee members—but Culver clearly established a method of encouraging people to support his personal candidacy, and his political stances, without forcing them to tie themselves to the Democratic Party itself. In a congressional district where registered Independents outnumbered both Republicans and Democrats, this was crucial. The Culver-Clark method had been contoured to meet the needs of the time. It was a method that worked well in an era of diffuse political allegiances.

ORGANIZED DEMOCRATS
— 149 —

To this difficult and detailed work of building a campaign organization, Culver added his own flair for campaigning, a crusading style that captured the imagination of many Second District voters. His broad appeal, achieved by his becoming known personally in the area, was an important ingredient in the campaign. For example, the Culver campaign had become a family affair. The candidate's wife Ann and his sister Kay walked for miles in tennis shoes, knocking on doors, even climbing aboard city buses, to distribute literature and talk with local residents. It was the first time in the Second District that an entire family had joined in the campaigning activities, and it reminded people of the approach made to national politics by the Kennedy family.

The constituents of the district were often reminded of the close personal and political ties binding the Culvers to the Kennedys. Several of the Kennedy family came to campaign for Culver. R. Sargent Shriver, brother-in-law of the Kennedys and director of the Peace Corps, visited the Democratic stronghold of Dubuque. Senator Edward Kennedy's wife Joan arrived shortly after Shriver departed. Although she also stopped in Dubuque, Maquoketa, and Cedar Rapids, Mrs. Kennedy most vividly displayed the magic of the Kennedy touch in Clinton County — a crucial area to the Culver campaign where few Democrats had ever done well. In Clinton, hundreds of citizens, including Republican Mayor Harold Domsalla, greeted Mrs. Kennedy at the airport. The Mayor proudly welcomed her "on behalf of the people of Clinton," and a highly partisan event was buried by the drama of a Kennedy visit. Even Clinton's Republicans bragged to local newspaper reporters of the autographs Joan Kennedy gave them, as well as of their moments of brief conversation with the national celebrity.[32] Indeed, the close ties between John Culver and

the Kennedy family were not forgotten by his supporters—
or by his Republican adversaries. When Ted Kennedy
barely escaped death in June 1964, after his twin-engine
plane had plunged into a Southampton, Massachusetts apple orchard, killing his staff assistant, a traditionally partisan Democratic newspaper, Cascade's *Pioneer-Advertiser,*
noted the assistant might well have been Culver, had he not
returned to run for Congress in Iowa: "It might be that
Culver is working under Zodiac or some good luck charm
and that his Second District constituents will take kindly to
his candidacy for the position of Representative in Congress and return him to Congress in that capacity."[33]

Culver's friendship with Kennedy added excitement to
the campaign and elevated what normally had been a local
political event to a national stature. The *Fayette County
Union and West Union Argo-Gazette* observed: "The [national] Democrat Party has evidenced more interest in...
the current political campaign than we can recall in a
quarter of a century."[34]

Though closely associated with the Kennedy family,
Culver's unique and aggressive style on the political stump
not only distinguished him from the Massachusetts politicians, but contrasted markedly to all previous congressional aspirants in the Second District as well. Face reddened with passion, Culver would bellow in a hoarse voice
from the hustings to spectators throughout northeast
Iowa. Sometimes delivering his speeches in stacatto bursts
as he beat his fists through the air, Culver often launched
harsh salvos at his opponent, transforming many of his
public appearances into political skirmishes. Armed with
facts and statistics telling the story of the district's current
relationship to the federal government, Culver claimed
Bromwell's stay in office had left the needs of the Second

ORGANIZED DEMOCRATS

District unmet. Culver promulgated his own hopes for the future, an outline of how federal programs might better the quality of life for the area's residents. "We need federal aid to education to improve educational opportunities; housing, health and recreation programs to improve the environment of both urban and rural America," said Culver.[35]

Culver's closest associates considered him to be more conservative than they were on many issues.[36] Culver labelled himself a "prudent progressive," neither liberal nor conservative, but rather one concerned about meeting obligations in humanitarian areas. He declared: "Government should not infringe upon the essential liberties of the individual, but can and must be made an instrument of positive action."[37] While calling for strong leadership in government and progressive programs at the federal level, Culver also circumscribed the limits of government authority.

As a moderate, Culver attacked his opponent on three major points: that Republican Bromwell was an "ultra conservative" whose early and continued support of Barry Goldwater showed him to be out of touch with the district (even Republican State Chairman Robert D. Ray had refused to support the Arizona senator for president at the Republican National Convention); that Bromwell had demonstrated a "negative" and "obstructionist" voting record against the programs needed by the Second District; and that Culver, as a member of the majority party in Congress, could quickly obtain the influence needed to boost Second District projects into the national legislative spotlight.

Sensing the Second District voters were less extreme than Barry Goldwater, Culver emphasized the ties between Bromwell and the Republican's presidential nominee.

A PARTY REBORN

Congressman John C. Culver campaigning with Senator Robert F. Kennedy and Governor Harold Hughes, 1966 (above), and discussing issues with Iowa farmers and a congressional delegation from Washington, D. C., 1966 (below).

ORGANIZED DEMOCRATS
— 153 —

Goldwater rewarded Bromwell's advocacy in two separate visits to the district. Culver used Goldwater's visits to define himself in contrast to his opponent. In his political advertisements, Culver pictured himself and Lyndon Johnson together on one side, with Bromwell and Goldwater paired on the other side. At a Labor Day picnic in Clinton, Culver tightened the Goldwater noose around Bromwell's neck with a series of charges, one rapidly following another. Speaking from a bandshell in a park before hundreds of onlookers seated on benches below, Culver bellowed a list of issues on which Bromwell and Goldwater agreed. Bromwell, without denying his support for his party's nominee, threw his own spiked barbs at Culver, touting the Democrat's ties to the Kennedy family.[38] The performance electrified the crowd. This summary appeared in a Cedar Rapids newspaper account: "The race developing for the congressional seat in the Second District is rapidly becoming as hot and turbulent as the weather we have been experiencing of late. Charges and counter-charges are being hurled like summer lightning bolts by the incumbent and the challenger and there seems no sign of letup until the rewarding November rains finally resolve the contest."[39]

Related to his anti-Goldwater rhetoric, Culver also campaigned against what he labelled as Bromwell's negative voting record of the past four years.[40] Throughout the district, in communities such as Postville, he reminded listeners that 20% of the town's population was elderly, eligible for the medicare programs Bromwell had opposed, at least in part, in Congress — and Culver told them of his own personal support for those programs. And when Culver talked to farmers in rural Fayette County, he reminded them that the federal feed-grains program would pump nearly two million dollars into that county alone, and over

16 million dollars into the eleven county area.[41] Charging the incumbent congressman had voted against provisions of the beneficial program, Culver told his audiences: "We must not be content to let a Republican congressman take credit for the gains made in this district by riding the waves of programs which he opposed."[42]

Finally, Culver appealed to the pragmatic instincts of Second District voters by claiming a Democrat, and only a Democrat, as a member of the majority rather than the minority party, had a better chance of obtaining those funds to which the district was potentially entitled. "It is vital for our district today that our congressman speak with a clear and forceful voice and as a member of the majority party in Congress," Culver said.[43]

Constantly moving through the district, Culver mixed his tough, open attacks on Bromwell with quiet jabs poked during private visits to local homes. The steady pressure from many directions he exerted on Bromwell forced the incumbent into a defensive posture during most of the campaign. Often stopping to respond to Culver's charges, Bromwell neglected to develop an effective strategy. He denied the specific charges made about his allegedly negative voting record. He sought to dispel Culver's "ultra conservative" label by reaching for the political middle ground. Bromwell often reminded audiences that he had supported the Civil Rights Bill. He chipped away at the Culver-Kennedy connection, calling his Democratic opponent a "carpetbagger" and a "Kennedy plant," themes suggestive of Dr. Feld's earlier campaign. Bromwell claimed Culver represented Eastern, not Midwestern values, and that Culver would turn Iowa into a "province of Massachusetts." Culver responded to the carpetbagger charge. He told voters he and Bromwell had attended the same elementary school, the same high school, and the same gradu-

ORGANIZED DEMOCRATS

ate school. He said both of them had left Iowa only for military service duties and to serve in government. "If Iowa isn't our home, Ann and I don't have one, and neither do thousands of others who went away to school, service or brief work experience before returning home," Culver stated.[44]

The Culver style instilled a new sense of drama in Second District Democrats. Now, during the final weeks of the campaign, the flurries of charges and countercharges doubtless received more public notice than the less visible organizational muscle the Culver camp had created in the course of the year. But the organization may well have given Culver the advantage needed to carry him to his slim victory over Bromwell. Even in a year of Democratic abundance, a total of only 8,171 votes cushioned Culver's victory. Those same eleven Second District counties handed Harold Hughes an 18,400-vote advantage in the gubernatorial race and provided President Lyndon B. Johnson with a landslide 50,600 votes over Barry Goldwater. The cities—the sites of the principal Culver-Clark network, the places visited by the national political celebrities on Culver's behalf, the locations where Culver had unleashed his most relentless criticisms of Bromwell—rewarded candidate Culver with the critical votes. In Clinton County, Culver's 900-vote majority made him the first Democratic congressional candidate to win there since 1938. Linn and Dubuque County voters also preferred Culver.[45]

CONGRESSMAN JOHN CULVER'S FIRST CAMPAIGN made him very visible throughout the Second District in a short time. Once elected, Culver maintained his high public profile, concentrating on servicing the needs of his eleven-county area. Between winning in November and taking the oath of office in January 1965 Culver stormed once more through

Richard C. Clark walking across the state of Iowa in his successful campaign for the United States Senate in 1972 (above) and relaxing after the victory (left)

the district, with Dick Clark at his side, holding meetings in each county to determine where federal programs were needed. During his first two-year term, Culver would visit 132 towns and cities, many of them more than once.[46] He underscored his focus on constituent service by committing key staff members to it. Unlike most other congressional administrative assistants, who worked with their bosses in Washington, D.C., Clark normally worked out of the Cedar Rapids Federal Building office. Close to the situation in Iowa, Clark carefully monitored community development projects. "Constituent service became a Culver trademark," the defeated James Bromwell later observed.[47]

In Washington, Culver contributed to one of the most remarkable legislative periods in the history of the nation. In 1964 and 1965, President Lyndon Johnson, emboldened by his overwhelming electoral victory, led the Congress to express a national purpose in clear and powerful terms. To attack racial discrimination, to launch a war on poverty, to reform the nation's system of education, to assure health care for the old and infirm, to stimulate the economy while attempting to improve the country's environment and protect its resources, even to make Southeast Asia "safe for democracy" — these became the goals of a nation seemingly determined to build a new society, a "Great Society."

These themes were optimistic in the speeches Culver delivered to each of 82 high schools in the district during his first term, encouraging citizens to increase their participation in governmental affairs.[48] He linked the accomplishments of the Congress to the aspirations of many Second District communities. He worked to shatter barriers that had existed since the New Deal between the federal government and the municipalities in his district's eleven counties. In these two years he brought to the area five cabinet officials, representatives from more than a dozen

A PARTY REBORN
— 158 —

federal departments and agencies, and three congressmen from the East to spend a weekend on local farms learning the legislative needs of northeast Iowa. In district-wide conferences, attended by more than 3,000 residents, Culver instructed federal officials to explain to his citizens those programs affecting agriculture, recreation and tourism, education, economic opportunity, and flood relief. He asked the officials to outline pending and existing legislation aimed at the needs of senior citizens, small businesses, and public works agencies.[49] By personally taking Great Society ideas and programs out of the committee rooms and hallways of Congress, and placing them in a Second District setting, Culver sometimes changed the outlooks of those who previously viewed such governmental initiatives with scepticism, if not contempt. A Republican newspaper, the Oelwein *Daily Register,* following one of the Congressman's conferences between constituents and federal officials, remarked: "Congressman Culver brought in a panel of experts to show what was available and how to get it fast. He performed a service to this district. . . . This is the kind of program under which we are now living and probably will continue to live during the lifetime of many of us. It used to be called socialism. . . . Now it's called government assistance seasoned with local planning."[50]

When communities had problems that could involve the federal government, Congressman Culver was on the scene asking questions and offering assistance. If emergency funding was needed to repair damage done by a Mississippi River flood in Guttenberg, if the Clayton County Civil Defense unit needed money from Housing and Urban Development, if district citizens wanted Postal Service support for a stamp to commemorate the Great River Road, or if the Dubuque flood control project sought backing

ORGANIZED DEMOCRATS
— 159 —

from the Army Corps of Engineers, Culver participated and insured active federal assistance.[51]

His style invited comparisons with his congressional predecessors. Leo Sullivan, 65, editor and publisher of another district newspaper, the Cascade *Pioneer-Advertiser,* concluded: "John Culver is a pretty good hired man for the Second District. There's as much difference between Culver and Talle as night and day. Talle never did anything. Culver has done a lot for the Second District and for the nation. Bromwell was an improvement over what we had been sending there to Washington, but Culver is an improvement over Bromwell."[52]

Indeed, in his first term Culver covered the traditional divisions that separated Democrats, Republicans, and Independents with a blanket of federal attention to local needs and aspirations. Looking back two years, Culver in 1966 told his audiences that he had helped to bring to the district more federal funds for local projects than had been paid in federal taxes. Nine new post offices had been constructed and 27 others remodeled in that short time span— more than in any other part of Iowa and more than the combined total of the previous decade in the district.[53] In smaller towns and bedroom communities, whose insufficient local taxes could not have supported such projects on their own, Culver's access to federal funding—his influence with U.S. Postmaster General Lawrence O'Brien, for example—stimulated civic pride and tied Culver's congressional service work visibly to the everyday lives of Second District citizens.[54] Cleo Berry of Sabula, writing in the Maquoketa *Jackson Sentinel,* summarized why John Culver would survive the 1966 GOP comeback: "It is downright silly to think that a Republican can do as much for this district under a Democratic administration as a Democrat can do."[55] Another local newspaper, the traditionally

Republican DeWitt *Observer,* presented accolades for Culver's pragmatic successes: "In an exceptionally short time Culver has become strongly entrenched. He has the voter identification of a twenty-year veteran. He has made the rounds. He knows the ropes. While his voting record may not bring joy to the hearts of Republicans, his office has apparently gotten the job done."[56]

Culver's ability to secure federal funds for many local projects, combined with his constant presence in the district, allowed him to use the slogan, "The Hardest Working Congressman We Ever Had" in his later campaigns. This was effective politics in a part of Iowa whose people, by instinct, valued independence, hard work, and accomplishment.

Beyond his personal abilities, of course, incumbent Congressman Culver carried with him the office-holder's inherent political and institutional advantages over possible challengers, advantages helpful in building a local political power base. His membership in the Democratic Party gave him priority access to federal funds for district projects. As a member of Congress, Culver enjoyed additional resources. His franking privilege allowed frequent mailings to the constituents and the press, describing his views on timely issues. Congress's radio and television recording facilities helped Culver relay word of his work in Washington to the folks at home.

In theory, all incumbents benefited from unequaled advantages over possible opponents. However, such devices alone had not guaranteed security for Culver's predecessors, Henry O. Talle, Leonard G. Wolf, or James E. Bromwell. Nor did mere accessibility to levers of power, campaign funds, and the public eye prevent four of Iowa's six Democratic congressmen elected in 1964 from losing their seats two years later. Rather, the style, the performance, and the reputation of John Culver, combined with the strength and depth of his expanding political and election-day operations, ensured his own political survival. When Mayor Robert M. L. Johnson of Cedar Rapids declared his candidacy for Culver's seat in 1966, the mayor attacked what he feared had become a strong relationship between local federal projects and the ballot box. This campaign is not "a campaign about sewers and bridges, post offices and parks or urban renewal," Johnson contended.[57] Congressman Culver continued on his way, however, and raced the mayor to take credit for city and district projects, while also pointing to instances where he had demonstrated leadership independent of Administration policies.

The war in Vietnam and Lyndon Johnson's war policies had fallen into public disfavor, but foreign policy did not dominate the campaign, although Culver largely agreed with the President. About the time Mayor Johnson accused Culver of being a rubber stamp for Administration programs, however, the President's portrait disappeared from the Congressman's campaign literature, and Culver began stressing the votes in Congress he had cast in opposition to Johnson.[58] As in 1964, Culver's 1966 campaign attracted a national audience. Both Edward and Robert Kennedy were greeted by wildly enthusiastic crowds when they visited the district on Culver's behalf during the first term.[59] In rebuttal, Mayor Johnson entertained former Vice-President Richard M. Nixon, House Minority Leader Gerald R. Ford, and Minnesota Congressman Walter N. Judd.

Culver used the perquisites of his office to overwhelm his challenger. In late October, 1966, as election day neared, Mayor Johnson waited in Cedar Rapids for word from Washington, D.C. concerning his city's $13 million urban renewal grant application under consideration. Meanwhile, Culver dashed home secretly with a copy of the grant confirmation notice in his hand. He stole the mayor's spotlight when he revealed the good news to the Cedar Rapids news media and citizens upon his surprising arrival. At the dedication ceremonies of the new Cedar Rapids post office building, Mayor Johnson, his campaign button stuck in his lapel, tried to take some of the credit for the project. But he and his button were lost in the crowd of luminaries up on the dais, luminaries whose presence had been carefully orchestrated in advance by Culver. Sitting on the stage with the mayor was Congressman Culver himself. Next to Culver sat U.S. Postmaster General, Democrat Lawrence O'Brien, who lauded Culver's work to secure funds for the new building. Behind them all hung large portraits of Postmaster O'Brien and President Johnson.[60]

Culver complemented his advocacy for local projects in the halls of Congress with an expanded election-day effort at home. "Campaign organizations are most crucial in the first two or three elections," stated Dick Clark, "until the candidate is known by nearly everyone, in which case the organization takes on a less central role."[61] Using a combination of telephone books and voter registration lists, scores of volunteers called every residence in the district's registration cities, not just in target precincts. Polling those who answered the calls about their political preferences, Culver and Clark got ready to bring all identified Democrats and favorable Independents to the polls. They expanded their door-to-door canvassing drives in the highly mobile precincts and uncovered unregistered Democrats whom they then registered to vote. Labor unions, especially the United Auto Workers, increased their aid in the canvassing and calling operations. Also, for the first time some rural precincts participated in the polling process, although the lack of voter registration requirements in those sectors hampered identification and election-day efforts.[62] Improved techniques provided Clark with better means to organize the increased political information into the more effective "walking decks" which volunteers used to locate Democratic households on election day. And an expanded campaign budget, though still well under $100,000, paid for the pamphlets, radio and television commercials, billboards, and special mailings used to persuade undecided voters up to the end of the campaign.[63]

On election day, the river-county voters, especially, responded to Culver's attention to their local needs. Clinton, Jackson, and Dubuque counties—three of the five counties bordering the Mississippi River—carried a Culver majority. Culver now joined veteran Neal Smith, the only other Democrat with a substantial organizational base, as the sole Iowa survivors of the 1966 GOP congressional sweep.

Congressman Culver's challenger in 1968, Republican Tom Riley of Cedar Rapids, proved to be his toughest opponent. A veteran state representative and state senator and successful attorney, Riley had a power base rivaling Culver's Linn County following. Culver and Clark responded to the contest by pushing their own organizational methods to their furthest possible limits. The plan of attack remained much the same as it had been in 1966, but with additional staff and increased campaign funds, Culver and Clark further refined and expanded their operation within the limits imposed by the card file and shoe box technology. They broadened phone canvassing in the cities to include more rural areas. Culver again used, but in greater quantities than before, the paraphernalia designed to give himself exposure throughout the district. Yard signs and bumper stickers, leaflets, billboards, radio and television commercials, all were a part of the Culver campaign. To date, "it was our most thorough campaign," remembered Clark later.[64]

The issues engaged by Riley and Culver stirred and mixed traditional loyalties to parties, to causes, and to the candidates themselves. As a "dove," Riley focused on the Vietnam War. He criticized the "domino theory" of Asian communism that ruled much State Department and Administration thinking. "Our involvement in Vietnam was a major foreign policy mistake and now I think we should get out," Riley said.[65] When Harold Hughes sided with the anti-war stance of Senator Eugene McCarthy of Minnesota at the Democratic National Convention in Chicago, and when in his own Senate race Hughes called Vietnam the "Nixon-Stanley war," Riley also applauded the Minnesota senator. "The dissent of Senator McCarthy and his supporters will have a lasting, positive effect on the nation," predicted Riley during his campaign. Culver opposed Riley's call for a unilateral, phased withdrawal of American troops from South Vietnam, but supported an end to the bombing of North Vietnam to test the lull in fighting as evidence of reciprocity.[66] The war issue split traditional alignments. Riley's surprising support of Senator McCarthy matched in shock value the sudden embrace given Culver's candidacy by former Republican Congressman James Bromwell.[67]

Riley and Culver both centered on the "guns and butter" question, so closely coupled with the war issue. That is, both men talked of the relationship between social programs and the defense budget as priorities in governmental spending. Riley's stunning position on the war was matched by Culver's own call for a reduction of the military budget, an increase in American non-military foreign

ORGANIZED DEMOCRATS
— 165 —

aid funding, and an increased domestic spending program for poverty. "The poverty program represents $1.7 billion a year for one-fifth of the American people and that is only half of what we spend in one month in Vietnam," said Culver. "This represents for the entire under-developed world less than we spend in one month in Vietnam."[68]

Iowans voted for stability rather than change in the 1968 congressional elections. All incumbents won re-election. The real surprise of Culver's Second District victory was its decisiveness. Expecting a close contest, Culver instead won 55% of the vote, his largest margin ever, by capturing seven of eleven counties in the district, all of the urban ones. "Our organization had been at its peak," explained Clark later.[69] The results convinced Culver and Clark that, with a strong organizational base, Democrats in Iowa could win even the most difficult of challenges. They looked ahead to the 1972 Senate race, thinking Culver might oppose Republican incumbent Jack Miller for the position. However, Culver and Clark knew the index-card and shoebox filing systems of the past would not be adequate for a statewide race. They hoped Culver's 1970 congressional race would produce a method of computerized operations to use in the 1972 Senate campaign.

Culver and Clark aimed to canvass by telephone all Democratic and Independent households in the registration cities and all voters in the smaller towns and rural areas. To finance the voter-identification and election-day preparations, they raised a war chest of over $130,000. Nearly $50,000 of those funds would pay for the canvassing expenses alone. To supplement the usual volunteer teams making thousands of phone calls, they hired 14 full-time staff members to coordinate the sweeping new district-wide calling program. They hired a business firm to create the needed lists for telephone canvassing by match-

A PARTY REBORN

ing and sorting names from voter registration lists in the cities and telephone directory listings from throughout the district. From the data gathered by the phone calls, combined with that accumulated from door-to-door canvassing in the most highly transient areas, the computers created lists of likely Culver supporters in every precinct. In the urban areas, volunteers assembled the computer lists into the traditional "walking decks" for election day. In the rural areas, staff and volunteers clustered into groups according to telephone exchange prefixes and made lists of voters to be called on election day.

The 1970 race between Culver and his latest challenger, Republican Cole McMartin, provided fewer fireworks than had some of the congressman's earlier contests. McMartin was a 21-year veteran of television news broadcasting in the Cedar Rapids area. Employed there by WMT-TV, McMartin, a slightly built and bespectacled man, was already well-known by Second District citizens. Private polls indicated that, outside of Clinton and Jackson counties, where WMT-TV had few viewers, McMartin was almost as familiar to voters as Culver before the campaign began.[70]

But McMartin's inexperienced political manner in a forum filled with cues and nuances different from the world of microphones, typewriters, and studio lights, contrasted sharply with the campaign style of Culver. Whereas Culver was often accompanied by groups of volunteers and staff who placed bumper stickers on cars and attended to logistical details, McMartin wandered around the district alone, driving himself here and there with appointment book in hand, sometimes hitting, often missing, important political opportunities. McMartin also seemed plagued with bad luck. As a member of the Cedar Rapids Optimist Club, McMartin attended one of its regular luncheons in the closing weeks of the campaign, only to find the featured speaker for the occasion to be his opponent John Culver. Trapped in the uncomfortable situation with no opportunity to respond to the congressman's remarks, McMartin sat silently through the speech as Culver confidently charted a course for his next term in Congress and lambasted positions taken by his helpless adversary.[71] Earlier, in front of the same group, McMartin had thrown a tough political punch. But not at his opponent. He took a swing at an important member of his own political party, Vice-President Spiro T. Agnew. "I think Agnew is probably overdoing it a little," McMartin had said, referring to Agnew's controversial political appearances in other parts of the nation. "I'd just as soon see him shut up between now and November 3."[72] The Vice-President, apparently, and Richard M. Nixon, too, had designs of their own that did not include taking advice from Cole McMartin. Two weeks after his Agnew statement, McMartin received a call from the White House about a visit the Vice-President intended to make to Cedar Rapids on October 23. There, McMartin was told, Agnew would personally attack John Culver's candidacy. When Agnew arrived at the Cedar Rapids airport, shouting over the heckling students surrounding him, he gave Culver perhaps the biggest boost of the 1970 campaign. The Vice-President called the Congressman "a textbook example of radical liberalism." Culver had anticipated the charge in advance and immediately responded with evidence showing he had supported the Nixon Administration on more votes in the previous term than several of Iowa's own Republican congressmen.[73] The appearance of Agnew embarrassed the state's Republicans and increased the intensity of Culver's support. The incumbent Democrat swept to an easy victory, increasing the margin he had built up over Tom Riley two years before.

A PARTY REBORN

The 1970 campaign organization had encountered numerous logistical difficulties in the experiment with the computers in the voter identification program, but Culver and Clark concluded the great expense had been worth the investment. They looked to the statewide situation, speculating on Culver's chances to unseat Republican Senator Jack Miller in 1972. Based on the model built in the 1970 campaign, the two men set out to organize an identification, registration, and election-day program. Opinion surveys had shown more Iowans now preferred the Democratic than the Republican Party, but the Democrats seemed to need prodding to register and vote in order to produce a majority on election day.

In 1971 Culver toured the state to test the political waters for his candidacy. Clark worked with Cliff Larson, the new state party chairman, to establish a branch organization, the Iowa Voters Committee, which, in turn, hired the Minneapolis consulting firm of Sherman-Valentine to create a statewide computerized voter identification system.[74] The initial goals of the program were, unknown to Clark and Larson, more ambitious than the consulting firm or they themselves could achieve. When Clark hired six field workers in the summer of 1971, he hoped they could, in turn, organize the volunteers in all 99 counties of the six congressional districts to canvass *every* Iowa household, and to identify the political party preferences of *all* Iowa voters. According to the plan, the $50,000 Sherman-Valentine program would provide computer-spewed lists for callers to use, with names grouped both by county and by telephone exchange numbers. Callers would record current address, voter-registration, and partisan-preference information for every voter in each household. Each Democratic county organization in the state would be asked to ensure enough volunteer participation to complete the entire canvass in twelve months' time.

ORGANIZED DEMOCRATS

Many problems prevented the completion of the canvass, and from June 1971 until July 1972 fewer than one-half of the anticipated calls were made. Delays in the processing schedules by Sherman-Valentine, numerous print-out errors, and a drastic over-estimation by Culver and Clark of the ability of volunteers and county organizations alone to carry the burden of the calling, all contributed to the program's shortcomings.[75]

In February of 1972, Culver "broke the Iowa Democrats' version of the Richter scale" with his announcement that he would not, after all, be a candidate for Jack Miller's Senate seat. Public opinion polls had indicated such a race would likely be close, but national Republican leaders hinted they would be keying on Miller's race, providing him with large campaign contributions difficult for a Democrat not widely known across the state to match.[76] No doubt, the disappointing and partial progress of the statewide identification program contributed to Culver's decision not to run.

Culver's early interest in the anticipated Senate race had caused other potential Democratic candidates to make different election plans. Dick Clark himself had geared up to run for Culver's Second District congressional seat. Now Clark received some encouragement to make his own bid for the Senate. As he explains:

> I had never once thought of running for the Senate, but when someone suggested I run I thought about it for a week and called people all over the state to get their opinions. By the end of the week I concluded that if I ran I would have no Democratic primary opponent, but that I probably could not win [the seat]. I vowed not to go one dollar into personal debt in the course of the campaign. And, I thought it would be a terrific experience, even if I didn't win.[77]

Within two weeks of Culver's surprise withdrawal, Dick Clark announced his own candidacy for the Senate. Don-

A PARTY REBORN
— 170 —

ning a tan safari suit and hiking boots, Clark walked across the state and waged a campaign combining homespun homilies with serious attacks upon incumbent Miller. Strongly backed by the urban press, Clark shattered Miller's liberal-moderate image when he accused the incumbent of catering to special interests in Washington, supporting an immoral war, and growing aloof from his home state, a state that had changed in his twelve-year absence. "In the middle of my walk, by the end of June," recalled Clark, "I could begin to feel things turn around in my favor."[78] While campaigning, Clark said of Miller:

> He wants Medicare, but he voted against it in 1965. He favors the $100 monthly minimum for Social Security recipients, but he voted against it. He wants some sort of no-fault insurance, but he voted to send it to committee and kill it. He favors an all-volunteer army, but he won't vote for the appropriation bill. He favors the 18-year-old vote, but he voted against the statute. He says he is for congressional reform, but he voted against eliminating the seniority system.[79]

Clark also adjusted the Sherman-Valentine program to aim for more modest goals. With time running out, he took short-cuts from the initial plan to call all homes in all counties. Now Republican households were expunged from the calling lists of registration cities. In some areas, only homes of registered Democrats were called. Crude as the new program appeared in some instances, Democrats for the first time had a means to identify, even if awkwardly, voters in nearly 80 counties—of which nearly 30 were completed in modified form by the fall of 1972.

Miller did not take Clark's candidacy seriously until it was too late. Clark stunned the state and the nation with a 55% to 45% margin over the incumbent. The magnitude of his victory was enough, perhaps, to call into question the central importance of Clark's organizational efforts. Some analysts believed the election represented more anti-

ORGANIZED DEMOCRATS

Miller sentiments than pro-Clark votes. But there were other indications that the party's first statewide identification and election-day strategies, even though only partially completed, had made a significant impact on the vote totals. Democratic presidential candidate George McGovern lost badly in Iowa, as he did in every state in the nation except Massachusetts. But in the 49 Nixon states, only in seven did McGovern do better than he did in Iowa. In congressional races, Democrat Edward Mezvinsky captured the First District seat from Republican incumbent Fred Schwengel, and the Iowa House delegation was now evenly divided, 3-3 (Iowa had lost one seat because of the 1970 census adjustments). In the state legislature, the Iowa Supreme Court had redrawn district lines and had dictated *all* Senate seats should be up for election *at once* — for the first time since the first session in 1846. The Democrats profited from the changes and made significant gains — winning eleven new Senate seats for a total of 22 out of the 50 possible seats. They also won seven new House positions, reducing the Republican majority from 62 to 56 members of the 100-seat House. In all, Democrats had made a very impressive showing in light of the debacle of their national ticket. Organizational efforts had played a significant role in these successes.

THE FINAL STEPS to solidify a strong Democratic Party organization came in 1973 and 1974. The Iowa Voters Committee of 1972, which had served as the nexus of the voter-identification efforts that year, had been disbanded when the Watergate hearings in Washington revealed that the Sherman-Valentine work had been partially financed with $50,000 in illegal corporate contributions from the Texas-based Associated Milk Producers, Incorporated.[80] To replace the Voters Committee, in anticipation of his

A PARTY REBORN

own upcoming Senate race, Harold Hughes and new State Chairman Tom Whitney joined the rest of Iowa's Democratic congressional delegation in 1973 to establish a new Voter Identification Program (V.I.P.).

When Hughes made his surprising decision to retire from the Senate at the end of his first term, John Culver immediately announced his candidacy for the seat and coordinated his campaign designs around the V.I.P. nucleus. Working with a two-year budget that approached $350,000, a staff of more than 30 persons, and a computer program improved from two years earlier, the party now organized virtually all areas of the state. There were even special efforts to organize "marginal" state legislative districts, with a separate budget of $50,000 in the 1974 program for additional work in those districts.

John Culver, in typically forceful campaign style, stormed from one county to the next, meeting head-on veteran campaigner and former Hughes opponent, David M. Stanley, in numerous debates. Culver made stump speeches to friendly partisan gatherings, reminding them of his success in the past. He reiterated the stories of how he and Dick Clark had transformed the Second District from a Republican-dominated area into a Democratic stronghold. He told of how they had "scrubbed up" the image of the party in those counties. And he pleaded for their assistance to conduct the expanded Voter Identification Program.

In this V.I.P. effort, it was hoped, *all* households in urban and rural areas alike would be canvassed by volunteer telephone pollsters and paid staff assistants. In the registration counties, now numbering 18, Culver aimed his own special program at increasing support among registered Independents. Paid workers called the Independent households and asked voters to list their *preferred* political

ORGANIZED DEMOCRATS

party. They asked those without a preference to name their choice for President should a hypothetical election be held between Edmund Muskie of Maine and Ronald Reagan of California. The Independents who named Reagan were omitted from further contacts. Culver's campaign also recruited several thousand Democratic "neighborhood leaders" and assigned them three tasks—first, to carry Culver literature to those households in their neighborhoods previously identified as Democratic-leaning Independents; second, to write 25 personal postcards to friends and relatives in support of Culver one week before election day; and, third, to participate in the general Democratic Party election-day efforts.

To perform the remainder of the polling work, congressional and state legislative campaign workers as well as county central committee volunteers called every remaining household in the state not called by Culver's separate Independent canvass. In these calls, pollsters elicited information about the voting habits of each resident. When questions revealed mistaken addresses or voter identities, pollsters corrected the appropriate computer cards so that later election-day "walking decks" would be accurate. When callers discovered unregistered voters in the course of their questioning, they immediately dispatched mobile registrars to those homes so residents might fill out the necessary registration documents. All of this information, from the urban and rural parts of Iowa alike, was gathered in the early autumn and the state's polled voters sorted by political preferences. Known Republicans would not be contacted again. Computers assembled the data, sorted it by geographical area, and printed out lists to be used for election-day drives. The lists resembled the ones used by Culver and Clark in their congressional campaign in 1970 and the Clark Senate campaign in 1972, but this time on a much vaster scale.

A PARTY REBORN

Democratic candidates for all offices and from all counties now joined Culver and built their own election strategies atop this broad organizational foundation. There was now little resemblance between the efforts of John Culver to secure a U.S. Senate seat and those of his predecessor E. B. Smith 14 years earlier. Newcomer Smith had scrambled about the state, aided by three unpaid, inexperienced friends. Culver, using his own trained and brilliant instincts and the valuable counsel of his continued close friend, Dick Clark, trouped through Iowa with no fewer than 20 paid campaign staff members. Smith had squeezed a $25,000 campaign budget to its limit and then had been humiliated in attempts to gain valuable public exposure without spending money. Culver also stretched his campaign treasury to its limits, but those now approached $400,000.

Though much larger and more complex than the initial attempts of the early 1950s, the 1974 Voter Identification Program of Iowa's Democratic Party resembled in certain ways the earliest Polk County operations. Then, Lex Hawkins, Mike Doyle, and others had canvassed Des Moines precincts on foot to identify and register voters. Now, in the year of Culver's Senate campaign, thousands of Democratic volunteers and paid workers throughout the state conducted hundreds of thousands of telephone interviews to poll *all* eligible, non-Republican voters, and mobile registrars scurried to the homes of those newly-identified, Democratic-leaning unregistered citizens. In the 1950s, on the Sunday before election day, Lex Hawkins had performed stirring incantations of rites and rituals in the excited atmosphere of packed Des Moines hotel ballrooms, rousing hundreds of workers to their tasks on the following Tuesday. Now in 1974 Democratic Party leaders, including Hughes, Clark, and Culver, flew to all the major

ORGANIZED DEMOCRATS

urban areas of the state on the pre-election Sunday to deliver those "fire-up" speeches to assembled party enthusiasts. And on election day, following the formulas of the first Polk County experiment, thousands of Democrats in all parts of Iowa now walked city streets, guided to the proper doorbells by computer printouts. Simultaneously, farm families called the previously identified Democratic and Democratic-leaning households in their rural townships to encourage their neighbors to go to the polls to elect Democratic candidates to office.

Just as the Polk County organizational efforts had ushered in greater political successes in the 1950s, so too did this completed statewide organization—an organization totally unmatched by the Republicans—reward the Democrats in 1974. Led by Culver, who would now join his former administrative assistant and campaign manager Dick Clark in Washington, D.C. to become the junior senator from Iowa, state Democrats also swept to impressive victories. Five Democratic congressional candidates, two more than in 1972, won. Only Charles Grassley, inheriting the Third District torch from 30-year GOP incumbent H. R. Gross, narrowly captured a House seat for the Republicans.

IT IS POSSIBLE, as Governor Robert D. Ray once asserted, that the Watergate scandals had "had a broad and devastating effect"[81] upon the Republican chances in the 1974 elections; that the Democratic victories of that year had been in part ephemeral, a public reaction against the Nixon Administration. But the degree to which Democrats had been successful at the local, state, and national political levels indicated a more widespread transformation had occurred.[82] Indeed, the creation of an effective and well-financed statewide Democratic organization had helped to

A PARTY REBORN

bolster those across-the-board gains which had been impossible to achieve only a few years earlier. Democratic fortunes would fluctuate from one election to the next in the years ahead. But in the newly competitive atmosphere of Iowa politics, it seemed unlikely that the Democratic Party would ever again become as weak and dispirited as it once had been.

NOTES

—I—
INTRODUCTION: IOWA POLITICS AND THE PROGRESSIVE INSTINCT

[1] Robert Dykstra, "Iowa: Bright Radical Star," in *Radical Republicans in the North: State Politics During Reconstruction,* ed. James C. Mohr (Baltimore, 1976), pp. 70-72.

[2] Michael Paul Rogin, *The Intellectuals and McCarthy: The Radical Specter* (Cambridge, Mass., 1967). Rogin discusses the movement for direct democracy in the Middle West in Chapter VII.

[3] Joseph Frazier Wall, *Iowa: A Bicentennial History* (New York, 1978), pp. 160-63.

[4] Fred E. Haynes, *Third Party Movements Since the Civil War: With Special Reference to Iowa* (Iowa City, 1916), p.125. Wall, *Iowa,* p. 163.

[5] Richard Hofstadter, *The American Political Tradition: And the Men Who Made It* (New York, 1948), p. 185.

[6] Wall, *Iowa,* pp. 163, 168.

[7] Leland L. Sage, *William Boyd Allison: A Study in Practical Politics* (Iowa City, 1956), p. 281.

[8] Wall, *Iowa,* p. 175.

[9] Rogin, *The Intellectuals and McCarthy,* p. 208.

—II—
URBANIZATION AND THE SILENT DEMOCRATS

[1] Republican Robert Blue had signed the right-to-work bill into law. *Cedar Rapids Gazette,* July 25, 1965.

[2] Even though the reported allowances are not necessarily accurate, in the 1950s the GOP's disclosed expenditures increased dramatically and surpassed the expenses reported by the Democrats.

Year	Republicans	Democrats
1950	$ 78,598	$ 81,000
1952	105,808	71,000
1954	120,000	75,000
1956	178,194	53,080
1958	134,086	17,285

See: *Des Moines Register* (hereafter abbreviated *DMR*): Dec. 6, 1950; Dec. 7, 1956; Nov. 27, 1958. *Iowa City Press-Citizen* (hereafter abbreviated *ICPC*): Dec. 2, 1958.

NOTES

[3]"...These appointments are devices [sic] rather than beneficial...." Letter from Donald J. Mitchell to John C. Culver, March 4, 1968. The Donald J. Mitchell Papers, Special Collections Department, University of Iowa Libraries, Iowa City, Iowa.

[4]Interview with Jake More (Oct. 8, 1976, Des Moines, Iowa); interview with Neal Smith (Sept. 16, 1976, Washington, D.C.).

[5]More, interview (Oct. 8, 1976).

[6]More, interview (Oct. 8, 1976). For Truman's own memoirs of the event, see Merle Miller, *Plain Speaking: An Oral Biography of Harry S. Truman* (New York, 1973), pp. 257-58.

Truman's speech had been aimed against Republican farm policies, which, through a new charter of the Commodity Credit Corporation, had made it more difficult for the government to acquire storage facilities for support operations. The Dexter speech was the major farm speech of Truman's campaign.

[7]Thomas D. Ungs, "The Republican Party in Iowa, 1946-1956," Diss. University of Iowa 1957, p. 172.

[8]Interview with Frank T. Nye (Aug. 10, 1976, Cedar Rapids, Iowa).

[9]*Smith-Lever Act, Statutes at Large,* XXXVIII (1914), 372.

[10]William J. Block, *The Separation of the Farm Bureau and the Extension Service: Political Issue in a Federal System* (Urbana, 1960), pp. 1-137.

[11]Interview with Kenneth Thatcher (Oct. 4, 1976, Cummins, Iowa).

[12]Thatcher, interview (Oct. 4, 1976); Block, *The Separation,* pp. 137-38, note 33; Charles W. Wiggins, "Interest Group Power Within State Legislative Systems: The Case of the Iowa Farm Bureau Federation," Diss. Washington University of St. Louis 1964, pp. 295-97.

[13]*DMR,* Sept. 4, 1956.

[14]*DMR,* Dec. 12, 1955; interview with Edris "Soapy" Owens (Oct. 12, 1976, Newton, Iowa); interview with Hugh D. Clark (Oct. 8, 1976, Des Moines, Iowa).

[15]*DMR,* Aug. 1, 1954.

[16]*DMR,* April 30, 1950.

[17]Wiggins, "Iowa Farm Bureau Federation," p. 87.

[18]Interview with Roswell Garst (Oct. 15, 1976, Coon Rapids, Iowa); see also Neal R. Peirce, *The Great Plains States: People, Politics, and Power in the Nine Great Plains States* (New York, 1972), p. 80.

Garst was a close personal friend of Henry A. Wallace (secretary of agriculture and Vice-President under Franklin D. Roosevelt) in the 1920s in Des Moines. Garst utilized Wallace's discovery of hybrid seed corn to launch an immensely successful business enterprise that marketed those grains. A few years later, he experimented with radical new feeding techniques for cattle and new fertilizing procedures. Finally, underscoring his real and symbolic importance to the rise of modern agriculture, Garst became, at the request of Nikita Khruschev, one of the nation's first farmers to visit the Soviet Union. Later he played host to the Russian leader at his Iowa farm so that Khruschev might view Garst's model operations first-hand.

NOTES

[19] Willard W. Cochrane and Mary E. Ryan, *American Farm Policy, 1948-1973* (Minneapolis, 1976), p. 5; J. S. Russell, "Iowa Farm-to-City Shift is Seen," *Iowa Farm and Home Register* (supplement to *Des Moines Sunday Register*), May 15, 1960.

[20] *Des Moines Sunday Register* (hereafter abbreviated *DMSR*), June 25, 1950.

[21] U.S. Department of Commerce, Bureau of the Census, *Nineteenth Census of the United States,* I, Part 17, *Population, 1970* (Washington, D.C., 1973), p. 17-7; idem., *Statistical Abstract of the United States: 1978* (Washington, D.C., 1978), p. 31.

[22] George B. Mather, *Effects of the Use of Voting Machines on Total Votes Cast: Iowa—1920 to 1960* (Iowa City, 1964), p. 16. Unpublished update by Mather and James C. Larew, January 1977. As explained in Mather's book (pp. 12-16), the urbanism score for each county "consists of the arithmetic mean of a series of up to ten individual percentage weights or bonuses...computed by dividing the combined population of cities over certain sizes by the total population of the county. We start with the combined population of the places over 500 population, then add extra percentages as the size of cities increases." In other words, this scale gives some weight to concentration of population within counties, and not just total of population figures. For an update through 1970, see below, chapter 5, footnote 5.

[23] Ronald C. Powers and Sue Meyers, *The Population Change of the Fort Dodge Area* (Ames, 1966), p. 3; Stewart L. Weiskind, "Settlement Changes and Spatial Behavior in Iowa: 1930-1960," Thesis Ohio State University 1969, p. 53.

[24] William Erbe, *Urbanization, Migration and Social Change: Iowa Enters the 1970s* (Iowa City, 1973), pp. 1-26; Weiskind, "Settlement Changes," p. 7; Ray M. Northan, "Declining Urban Centers in the United States: 1940-1960," *Annals of the Association of American Geographers,* 53 (March 1963), 50-59.

[25] Gerald L. Nordquist, "A Summary of Economic and Social Developments in Iowa," *Iowa Business Digest,* 31 (Aug. 1960), 8; John R. Schmidhauser, *Iowa's Campaign for a Constitutional Convention in 1960* (New York, 1963), p. 1; Wiggins, "Iowa Farm Bureau Federation," p. 82; Thomas D. Ungs, "The Republican Party in Iowa, 1946-1956," pp. 33-34.

[26] Wiggins, "Iowa Farm Bureau Federation," p. 76.

[27] Interview with James Risser and George Anthan, reporters for the Washington Bureau of *Des Moines Register* (Sept. 16, 1976, Washington, D.C.).

[28] Paul T. David, *Party Strength in the United States, 1872-1970* (Charlottesville, Va., 1972), p. 43. David classifies the state's shift as having occurred between 1932 and 1970. According to his analysis, Iowa was joined in similar realignments by Massachusetts, Connecticut, Pennsylvania, Illinois, Wisconsin, Minnesota, Idaho, and Washington.

[29] Several studies have demonstrated such voting patterns. Although each study has used various definitions of "urbanization" and "partisan preference," the trends emerge clearly in all these works: Samuel Lubell, *The Future of American Politics,* 3rd ed. (New York, 1965), pp. 165-73 (years 1916-48); Harlan

NOTES

Hahn, *Urban-Rural Conflict: The Politics of Change* (Beverly Hills, Ca.,1971), pp. 22-26, 73-76, 86-97 (1928-64); Thomas D. Ungs, "The Republican Party in Iowa, 1946-1956," pp. 80-83 (1946-56); Richard Bender and Ben Benzene, "The Computerized Statistics Collection Program of Iowa, 1966-1970," unpublished study by the Democratic Party of Iowa.

[30] Mather, *Effects of the Use of Voting Machines*, p. 31. The measurement of partisanship for each election year was computed by taking the arithmetic mean of the percent of the electorate voting for each party's candidate for president, senator, and governor in that election and the preceding two elections. For update through 1970, see chapter 5, footnote 5. See also Jerrold L. Buerer, "Urbanization and Political Party Competition in the State of Iowa," in *Urbanization, Migration and Social Change*, pp. 55-66; and David Gold and John R. Schmidhauser, "Urbanization and Party Competition: The Case of Iowa," *Midwest Journal of Political Science*, 4 (1960), 63-65. Each of these two studies uses political tendency measurements based upon the number of elective offices held by each party after each election, rather than upon proportion of votes cast for each party. This, in particular, explains how Gold and Schmidhauser could conclude that there existed no relationship between urbanization and partisan preference.

[31] Ruth Suckow, *Some Others and Myself: Seven Stories and a Memoir* (New York, 1932), pp. 200-01.

[32] Correlation coefficients were computed by taking the partisan preference measurements (that is, the arithmetic mean of the percent of the two party vote cast Republican for president, senator, and governor in that election and the preceding two elections) against education, median income (actually median income for a family of four), and median age figures procured from U.S. Census data for each of Iowa's 99 counties. Because census data is computed on a decennial basis, the author assumed constant rates of change and estimated figures for two-year intervals by means of linear interpolation. In the final step, linear regressions for each election year were computed, resulting in the displayed correlation coefficients (see Table 4 below). Such coefficients are a measurement of the degree to which the regression equations produced accurate predictions. The uniformly low values indicate a virtual absence of linear relations between voting behavior and the tested variables. (These values have less than a .01 probability of having occurred by chance.)

The Relationship Between
Republican Partisan Preference
and
Male Education, Female Education,
Median Income and Age in Iowa, 1940-1970

CORRELATION COEFFICIENTS

NOTES

	male education vs. GOP Preference	female education vs. GOP Preference	median income vs. GOP Preference	Age vs. GOP Preference
1940	.11	.06		
1942	−.01	.00		
1944	−.21	−.14		
1946	−.18	−.09		
1948	−.20	−.08		
1950	−.16	.04	−.17	.23
1952	−.19	.03	−.24	.21
1954	−.18	.03	−.24	.16
1956	−.13	−.01	−.24	.08
1958	−.07	−.01	−.22	.06
1960	−.09	−.06	−.24	.08
1962	−.17	−.10	−.25	.18
1964	−.24	−.17	−.21	.19
1966	−.29	−.20	−.16	.22
1968	−.31	−.27	−.12	.23
1970	−.24	−.32	−.08	.24

Source: Mather, *Effects of the Use of Voting Machines.*

[33] *DMSR,* "The Iowa Poll, Iowans' Top Concerns: Schools and Roads," Jan. 4, 1959; *DMR,* Dec. 30, 1956.

[34] *DMSR,* "The Iowa Poll, Cities Favor Liquor-by-Drink; Towns and Farms Oppose," May 15, 1952.

[35] Interview with Fred Schwengel (Aug. 18, 1976, Kansas City, Missouri). Schwengel served as a member of the Iowa General Assembly and later as a member of Congress as a Republican.

[36] Wiggins, "Iowa Farm Bureau Federation," p. 119.

[37] Interview with Robert Johnston (Jan. 10, 1977, Chicago, Illinois).

[38] Schmidhauser, *Constitutional Convention,* pp. 1-3. As Schmidhauser notes, farm insurgents in 1920 won, through statewide referendum, the right to hold a constitutional convention, but it was never held—unusual and unconstitutional though it was—after the General Assembly placated them with their desired legislation: statutes which legalized the withholding of farm produce.

[39] *DMSR,* Dec. 30, 1956.

[40] *DMSR,* "The Iowa Poll, New High Vote for Reapportionment," Feb. 17, 1957.

−III−
STIRRINGS IN POLK COUNTY: DEMOCRATS OF THE 1950s

[1] Interview with Michael Doyle (Oct. 13, 1976, Des Moines, Iowa).

[2] Interview with Wade P. Clarke (Oct. 14, 1976, Des Moines, Iowa); interview with Neil Smith (Feb. 8, 1980, Washington, D.C.).

NOTES
— 182 —

³Clarke, interview (Oct. 14, 1976).

⁴Robert L. Johnston later served as the Midwest Regional Director for the International UAW in Chicago, Illinois.

⁵Doyle, interview (Oct. 13, 1976).

⁶As late as 1976, Polk County voter-registration figures varied markedly from the state pattern or that of any other urban county. For example, in 1976, roughly one-third of all voters were registered independent while most urban areas showed slightly higher figures. For Polk County, however, only about 15% of the voters registered as Independents. The reason for this apparently inexplicable anomaly may be found in the following analysis by Arthur Hedberg, Jr., former Polk County chairman and long-time party worker: "The lower percentage of registered Independents has something to do, I think, with a registration gimmick that we used successfully. We'd ask the Independents on our canvasses, 'For the purpose of voting in the *primary* which party will you identify with?' Of course, a person in this state has to declare party allegiance to vote in the party primaries. And if a person would say, 'I'm an Independent,' we'd still pursue them with, 'Yes, I understand, but for the party primary, which party will you register with?' We got lots of Independents to register that way, and many of them with the Democratic Party." Interview with Arthur Hedberg, (Oct. 7, 1976, Des Moines, Iowa).

⁷Hedburg, interview (Oct. 7, 1976); *Des Moines Register* (hereafter abbreviated *DMR*), Oct. 6, 1952; *Cedar Rapids Gazette* (hereafter abbreviated *CRG*), March 24, 1956; *Des Moines Tribune* (hereafter abbreviated *DMTrib*), Oct. 12, 1956.

⁸Interview with Robert L. Johnston (Jan. 6, 1976, Chicago, Illinois).

⁹Hedburg, interview (Oct. 7, 1976).

¹⁰Thomas G. Ryan, "The Early Years of the Iowa Democratic Revival, 1950-1956," unpublished paper presented to the Conference of Iowa College Teachers of History, Oct. 14, 1978, Cedar Falls, Iowa, p. 12.

¹¹*Iowa Official Register,* 46 (1955-56) (Des Moines, Iowa, 1955), 348, 352.

¹²Letter from Neal Smith to Donald J. Mitchell, Dec. 17, 1954. The Donald J. Mitchell Papers, Special Collections Department, University of Iowa Libraries, Iowa City, Iowa.

¹³*CRG,* Nov. 9, 1950; *Council Bluffs Nonpareil,* Nov. 8, 1950.

¹⁴*CRG,* April 1, 1951.

¹⁵*CRG,* April 1, 1951.

¹⁶*DMR,* May 28, 1951.

¹⁷*CRG,* Aug. 1, 1954.

¹⁸Johnston, interview (Jan. 6, 1976); *DMTrib,* Feb. 6, 1953; *CRG,* Aug. 1, 1954.

¹⁹"Over the Anthills," *Time,* Oct. 22, 1956, p. 24.

²⁰*DMR,* July 18, 1954; Oct. 2, 1954; Oct. 27, 1954.

²¹*DMR,* July 21, 1954.

²²*DMR,* July 21, 1954; *CRG,* Aug. 1, 1954.

NOTES

[23] *DMR,* Sept. 26, 1954, Oct. 10, 1954, Oct. 25, 1954; *CRG,* Oct. 17, 1954.
[24] *DMR,* Nov. 4, 1954.
[25] *DMR,* Oct. 17, 1954, Feb. 28, 1955, March 29, 1955, April 20, 1955; "Over the Anthills," pp. 24-26.
[26] *DMR,* July 21, 1955. One prominent Republican, Jack Miller, who would later serve two terms in the United States Senate, viewed the change of labor allegiances from his vantage in the Iowa Senate in 1955. In retrospect, Miller speculates that if the legislature had been properly reapportioned, there might not have been an alignment between labor groups and the Democratic Party in Iowa: "Essentially, I am convinced that had there been earlier reapportionment of the state legislature, the Republican losses would not have occurred—because the extra votes (which in those days would still have come from Republican members) would have brought different results—more to the liking of a majority of the voters. Extra Republican votes from the more populous areas having large labor voting blocs would have been more responsive to modification (not repeal) in the labor laws. Outright repeal of the 'right-to-work' law was not necessary to secure the support of half the labor union vote (labor union leaders to the contrary notwithstanding). It was not mere coincidence that the state president of the AFL-CIO, Ray Mills, changed his registration from Republican to Democrat in 1955, although he still claimed to vote for the man." Interview with Jack Miller (Sept. 12, 1976, Washington, D.C.).
[27] *DMR,* Aug. 8, 1955.
[28] *DMR,* Aug. 1, 1954.
[29] *DMR,* Aug. 11, 1955.
[30] *CRG,* Dec. 19, 1955.
[31] *DMR,* May 28, 1956.
[32] Interview with Edris "Soapy" Owens (Oct. 12, 1976, Newton, Iowa). Owens, who ten years later would lead his union out of the merged AFL-CIO, assesses the role played by Mills: "Mills was never a strong political leader in the labor movement. He followed the Samuel Gompers approach and he felt he could do more with labor's interests if he kept good relations with the Republicans. But there was no one in that party to listen to labor."
[33] *DMR,* Dec. 12, 1955, Jan. 12, 1956; *DMTrib,* June 27, 1956.
[34] Iowa Federation of Labor, AFL-CIO, *Proceedings of the First Annual Convention of the Iowa Federation of Labor AFL-CIO, June 27-28, 1956* (Des Moines, 1956), p. 12.
[35] *DMR,* June 29, 1956; *CRG,* Dec. 31, 1956.
[36] Interview with Tom Dawson (Sept. 15, 1976, Washington, D.C.).
[37] Willard W. Cochrane and Mary E. Ryan, *American Farm Policy, 1948-1973* (Minneapolis, 1976), p. 33.
[38] Letter from Donald J. Mitchell to Adlai E. Stevenson, Feb. 1, 1956. Mitchell Papers.
[39] "Over the Anthills," p. 25.
[40] The majority of Iowans by March 1954 favored legalization of liquor-by-

NOTES

the-drink. The watershed community size for opinion on this subject hovered near population size 2,500. Those smaller than that were against alteration of the statute, while those in larger communities favored changes in the liquor laws. *DMSR*, "The Iowa Poll, Poll Gives Narrow Margin to Liquor by Drink in Iowa," March 28, 1954.

[41]"Over the Anthills," p. 26; *DMSR*, Sept. 9, 1956; *DMR*, Oct. 21, 1956, Nov. 4, 1956, Nov. 8, 1956.

[42]Interview with Herschel C. Loveless (Sept. 15, 1976, Washington, D.C.).

[43]Thomas D. Ungs, "The Republican Party in Iowa, 1946-1956," Diss. University of Iowa 1957, p. 245.

[44]*DMR*, July 29, 1958; *CRG*, July 29, 1954; John R. Schmidhauser, *Iowa's Campaign for a Constitutional Convention in 1960* (New York, 1964), p. 5.

[45]*DMR*, July 23, 1956; July 27, 1956; July 28, 1956; Aug. 1, 1956.

[46]The district delegates were selected by county conventions, and county delegates were nominated in precinct meetings and then elected on the primary ballot in each precinct. At that time, each Iowa political party held two state conventions in presidential years. The first convention selected delegates (or more often, confirmed those selections made by party leaders) to the national convention, who in turn elected the state party's national committeeman and committeewoman. The second state convention elected as members to the State Central Committee two delegates from each congressional district.

[47]Loveless, interview (Sept. 15, 1976).

[48]*Davenport Times-Democrat* (hereafter abbreviated *DavTD*), Aug. 8, 1958.

[49]Interview with Donald R. "Duke" Norberg (Sept. 16, 1976, Washington, D.C.).

[50]*DavTD*, July 24, 1958, Aug. 8, 1958; *CRG*, July 28, 1958; *DMR*, July 29, 1958.

After More's ouster, Iowa Democratic leaders worked strenuously to prevent a possible comeback. Seventeen years earlier More had founded the Midwest Conference, a group that represented many central states and whose planned purpose was to advise national legislators of state needs. As chairman of that conference, Jake More had a podium from which he could occasionally gain the national spotlight.

When More was dumped from the state party chairmanship, Iowa leaders were fearful he would use the Midwest Conference as a springboard back into Iowa politics. As a result, they worked closely with Midwest Conference members Neil Staebler (Michigan State Chairman), Paul Butler (National Democratic Chairman), Frank Theis (National Committeeman from Kansas), and Thomas Quimby (National Committeeman from Michigan) to rid More of his conference chairmanship as well. The initial constitution of the Midwest Conference, written largely by More, had stipulated that any present or past party leader could be a member of the conference; thus, even though he no longer retained his state chairmanship, More held onto his conference post. At two meetings in 1958 (the first in Milwaukee in March, the second in Kansas City in September) Theis,

Quimby, and Staebler broke away from the More conference. They organized their own meeting, calling themselves the official Midwest Conference, and secured recognition as such, via Butler, from the National Democratic Committee. They immediately wrote a constitution that stipulated that all conference members must be currently elected officials. Iowans, too, had been instrumental in this final ouster. Duke Norberg, Donald J. Mitchell, and Governor Loveless all attended the decisive Kansas City meeting.

Effectively barred from a position of leadership for the first time in 20 years, More attempted to run for position as a delegate to the Democratic National Convention of 1960. Many speculated that, if elected, he would run for Donald J. Mitchell's post as national committeeman. But More failed on four successive roll call votes to win the convention nod from the Seventh District delegates.

See: *DMR,* Sept. 12, 1959, Sept. 14, 1959, Sept. 15, 1959. Letter from Donald J. Mitchell to Donald R. "Duke" Norberg, June 17, 1959; letter from Frank Theis to Donald J. Mitchell, Sept. 28, 1959; letter from Donald J. Mitchell to Donald R. "Duke" Norberg, Sept. 28, 1959; letter from Donald J. Mitchell to Thomas Quimby, Sept. 28, 1959. Mitchell Papers.

[51]*CRG,* July 21, 1958; *DMR,* July 22, 1958, Sept. 13, 1958.

[52]Norberg, interview (Sept. 16, 1976).

[53]The Hoffa ties had received some publicity already. The Senate Labor Rackets Committee in Washington had heard testimony to the effect that Hoffa had made payments to More through Teamster Barney Baker, a Hoffa lieutenant. But the charges in the Republican press release were more fantastic; they intimated that the Teamster money had been gained by the union through kidnap ransom schemes. Apparently More had been friendly with Teamster Baker, but further allegations could not be substantiated.

See also: *DMR,* Sept. 13, 1958, Sept. 28, 1958; *DMTrib,* Sept. 25, 1958; *DavTD,* Sept. 28, 1958; *Omaha World-Herald,* Oct. 16, 1957; *CRG,* Nov. 2, 1958.

[54]*DMSR,* "The Iowa Poll: Why Iowans Think Loveless was Re-elected," Jan. 4, 1959.

[55]*Iowa Official Register* 48 (1959-1960) (State of Iowa, 1959), pp. 327, 366-67, 377-79; *ICPC,* Nov. 3, 1958; *DMTrib,* Nov. 5, 1958; *DMR,* Nov. 6, 1958, Nov. 9, 1958; *DavTD,* Nov. 7, 1958.

[56]This discussion concerning legislative reapportionment is based on the following sources not directly cited: John C. Culver, "Legislative Apportionment: The Iowa Story," B.A. Honors Thesis Harvard College 1954; Frank Nye, "Reapportionment in Iowa," *The Palimpsest,* 45 (June 1964), 241-72; Charles W. Wiggins, "Constitutional Convention Issue in Iowa, 1960," *Annals of Iowa,* 3rd ser., 40 (Winter 1970), 171-90; *Facts and Opinions About the Shaff Plan* (Iowa City, 1963).

[57]Charles W. Wiggins, "Interest Group Power Within State Legislative Systems: The Case of the Iowa Farm Bureau Federation," Diss. Washington University of St. Louis 1964, p. 116.

NOTES
— 186 —

⁵⁸Interview with Robert Fulton (Dec. 8, 1976, Waterloo, Iowa).
⁵⁹Wiggins, "Iowa Farm Bureau Federation," p. 233.
⁶⁰Wiggins, "Iowa Farm Bureau Federation," p. 87. The IMA opposed the convention because it feared the convention would write a union shop amendment into the state constitution, while the IFBF was afraid that such a convention would reapportion the farm group out of power.
⁶¹Wiggins, "Iowa Farm Bureau Federation," pp. 284-85.
⁶²On the labor issue, Republicans led by State Senator Jack Miller shrewdly divided the Democrats into rural and urban camps. To that point, Democratic leaders had openly charged that the GOP had prevented progressive steps to be taken on the labor question. However, when Miller, using unusual parliamentary procedures, forced two labor bills onto the floors of both chambers, Democrats factionalized. One of the bills, which would have repealed the right-to-work law completely, lost when 15 Democrats in the House switched ranks to join the Republicans. The vote was 74-33 against passage.
See also: *DMTrib*, Jan. 21, 1959, Feb. 3, 1959; *DavTD*, Feb. 1, 1959, Feb. 17, 1959; *DMR*, Feb. 5, 1959, Feb. 13, 1959.
⁶³Schmidhauser, p. 17; *CRG*, July 21, 1960, July 22, 1960; *DMR*, July 20, 1960, July 22, 1960.
⁶⁴With Martin's sudden departure, six Republican candidates entered the primary race for the Senate seat. None garnered the 35% plurality required by law to secure the nomination; for the first time in Iowa Republican history, the state convention selected the candidate. Miller's tireless work to collect convention votes—he added another 2,000 miles to the 62,000 miles traveled visiting key convention delegates—rewarded him with a narrow victory.
See also: *CRG*, July 22, 1960, July 24, 1960.
⁶⁵Louis Harris and Associates, Inc., Poll #866, "A Study of the Race for U.S. Senator in Iowa," Sept. 30, 1960, p. 18. The Herschel Loveless Papers, Special Collections Department, University of Iowa Libraries, Iowa City, Iowa.
⁶⁶*DMR*, Oct. 11, 1960; *CRG*, Jan. 20, 1960; *DMTrib*, Nov. 9, 1960; *Iowa Official Register*, 49 (1961-1962) (Des Moines, Iowa, 1961), 364.
In a letter to Maurice Rosenblatt of the Committee for an Effective Congress, Loveless attempts to assess the impact of religious beliefs on the election: "People who had remained fairly reasonable in their outlook up to that point two weeks before the election suddenly yielded to their fear and prejudices and so great was their determination to defeat the Democratic Presidential candidate, that they voted a straight ticket to be sure that their ballot would not be disqualified by some error in scratching.
"My opponent for the Senate, who is a Catholic, printed two sets of literature—one for Catholics and one for Protestants. As a consequence, at least one-third of the people who voted for him were unaware that he was a Catholic. They assumed that a person named 'Miller' would be a German Lutheran." Loveless to Rosenblatt, Nov. 28, 1960. Loveless Papers.

NOTES

—IV—
THE DEMOCRATS REBORN: THE RISE OF HAROLD HUGHES

[1] Norman H. Nie, Sidney Verba, and John R. Petrocik, *The Changing American Voter* (Cambridge, Mass., 1976), *passim.*

[2] *Des Moines Tribune* (hereafter abbreviated *DMTrib*), March 4, 1961; *Des Moines Register* (hereafter abbreviated *DMR*), March 7, 1961; *Iowa Official Register,* 49 (1961-1962) (Des Moines, 1961), 375-76.

[3] *Cedar Rapids Gazette* (hereafter abbreviated *CRG*), June 29, 1962.

[4] *DMR,* Nov. 2, 1962.

[5] In Herschel Loveless's first administration, unfair practices had been discovered in the Republican-dominated Commerce Commission. Harold Hughes, as an independent trucker, had gone directly to the Capitol to complain to Loveless of Commerce Commission operations. Loveless encouraged Hughes to run for the Commission himself. Hughes did, and in 1958 was elected. In 1960, he ran for the Democratic nomination for governor against Jake More ally Edward M. McManus. McManus won the primary, but lost in the general election to Norman Erbe. See: Harold E. Hughes and Dick Schneider, *The Man from Ida Grove: A Senator's Personal Story* (Lincoln, Va., 1979), pp. 122-25, 135-36, 138.

[6] *Des Moines Sunday Register* (hereafter abbreviated *DMSR*), May 6, 1962.

[7] *DMR,* Oct. 17, 1962, Nov. 4, 1962, Nov. 8, 1962; *Iowa City Press-Citizen* (hereafter abbreviated *ICPC*), Nov. 5, 1962.

[8] *DMR,* Sept. 7, 1973.

[9] *DMR,* July 16, 1971.

[10] Nie, Verba, and Petrocik, pp. 14-42.

[11] Ibid., p. 178.

[12] Ibid., p. 166.

[13] Interview with Edward Campbell (Oct. 7, 1976, Des Moines, Iowa).

[14] Vance Bourjaily, "The Governor from Ida Grove," *New York Times Magazine,* Feb. 26, 1967, p. 35.

[15] Hughes would create a national stir in 1971 when, as an unannounced candidate for the Presidency, he would reveal to reporters that while he had been Iowa's governor he had attended seances at which he had spoken, he believed, to his deceased brother through a medium. Hughes and Schneider, pp. 296-98; Nick Thimmesch, "The Lord and Harold Hughes," *Saturday Evening Post,* June/July, 1974, p. 43.

[16] Thimmesch, p. 44.

[17] Hughes organized prayer groups composed of notable Washington, D.C. figures including Charles Colson, former White House staff person in the Nixon Administration.

[18] James M. Wall, "A Senator's Faith and Vocation," *Christian Century,* Sept. 26, 1973, pp. 931-32.

[19] James Deakin, "1972? Well, let's see now...," *Esquire,* Feb. 1970, pp. 139-41. Paul R. Wieck, "The Presidential Candidacy of Harold Hughes: For God and Country," *New Republic,* May 15, 1971, pp. 19-24.

NOTES

[20] Bourjaily, p. 35.

[21] Frank T. Nye, "The 60th General Assembly of Iowa," *The Palimpsest,* 44 (Oct. 1963), 467-68.

[22] Harlan D. Hahn, *Urban-Rural Conflict: The Politics of Change* (Beverly Hills, Calif., 1971), pp. 141-43; Merle Fleming Full, "Until Hell Freezes Over," (unpublished analysis of Harold E. Hughes as governor of Iowa), 1968, p. 16.

[23] Full, p. 16.

[24] Nye, "The 60th General Assembly of Iowa," p. 483.

[25] Neal R. Peirce, *The Great Plains States: People, Politics, and Power in the Nine Great Plains States* (New York, 1972), p. 95.

[26] Even though the temporary plan increased urban representation, 47% of the electorate could still elect a majority of the representatives and 39% could elect a majority of senators.

The process of reapportionment of the Iowa legislature extended over a ten-year period and involved a number of court suits and counter suits. In 1962 the *Baker v. Carr* decision of the U.S. Supreme Court ruled that it had, and therefore the lower federal courts had, jurisdiction in matters involving state legislative reapportionment. Shortly thereafter, in the *Reynolds v. Sims* decision of 1964, another historic decision of the high court determined that state legislatures must be apportioned on a population or "one-man, one-vote" basis. Thus, plans like the Shaff Plan, based on a "federal" analogy, were clearly unconstitutional. And so ruled the federal district court in Iowa when it agreed with the Iowa Federation of Labor's objection that the temporary plans established by special session of the Iowa legislature in November 1964 were correct.

The 1965 session of the Iowa legislature drew up new plans which reflected biases of the urban delegations, but stipulated that all such urban seats would be elected at large, rather than by sub-districts. Republicans were successfully locked out of the legislature in the urban areas and they approached the courts. In April 1966, the Iowa Supreme Court stipulated that no at-large delegations could be elected.

In an attempt to meet the guidelines of the Iowa court, the 1967 legislature appointed an outside commission to propose equitable reapportionment plans. In 1968, the state passed by majority vote the permanent reapportionment amendment, first initiated by the 1965 legislature, which called for a House no larger than 100 members; a Senate no larger than 50 seats; apportionment of both chambers according to population, not area; automatic redistricting by the courts if the legislature proved unable to reapportion itself; and the right of any voter to challenge a reapportionment plan by appealing directly to the Iowa Supreme Court.

In 1969, the legislature took on the task of implementing the permanent reapportionment amendment of 1968. Now Republicans controlled both chambers and, against warnings levelled by the Supreme Court, allowed their biases to show as they drew new district lines which were designed to "save" Republican incumbents. Upon adjournment of the 1969 session, Clark Rasmussen immedi-

NOTES
— 189 —

ately filed suit in court against Robert Ray and the State of Iowa, asserting that the legislature had not followed the guidelines drawn up by the court. In its decision of *Rasmussen v. Ray*, the high court concurred with Rasmussen and called the existing plan unconstitutional, yet refused to call off upcoming elections based on that plan.

The "unconstitutional session" of the Iowa legislature in 1971 drew up new boundaries, but upon adjournment five groups—including the League of Women Voters, the UAW, the IFL, and the Democratic Party of Iowa—filed three separate suits with the Supreme Court, each challenging the just-passed plan. The arguments paralleled the Rasmussen complaints of two years earlier, and again the high court concurred. This time, however, using power given in the 1968 constitutional amendment, the court itself took the responsibility to draw up the new plans.

On January 14, 1972, in the opinion of many a memorable day in Iowa constitutional and political history, the Supreme Court of Iowa unanimously declared the 1971 apportionment plan unconstitutional and commanded the legislature to postpone the 1972 primary election date so that the justices might draw up new district lines after careful study.

On March 31, 1972, the court completed its study and the new plan, which contained population deviations substantially below those in the 1971 plan, was put into effect. The 1971 reapportionment plan had contained maximum population deviations of 3.8% between the largest and smallest House districts and 3.2% between the largest and smallest Senate districts. In contrast, the population deviations in the new plan were considerably lower—less than .1% in both chambers. Iowa's legislature was the most equitably apportioned in the country.

See: Charles Wiggins, "The Post World War II Legislative Reapportionment Battle in Iowa Politics," in *Patterns and Perspectives in Iowa History*, ed. Dorothy Schwieder (Ames, 1973), pp. 418-30.

[27]*DMTrib*, Nov. 8, 1962; Nov. 10, 1962; Nov. 19, 1962.

[28]Interview with Cliff Larson (Oct. 13, 1976, Ames, Iowa); interview with E. B. Smith (Sept. 21, 1976, College Park, Maryland); *DMR*, June 20, 1961, June 22, 1961, July 2, 1961.

[29]Interview with Tom Dawson (Sept. 15, 1976, Washington, D.C.); *DMTrib*, Oct. 9, 1962.

[30]E. B. Smith, interview (Sept. 21, 1976).

[31]*DMR*, Sept. 16, 1962, Oct. 28, 1962, Nov. 10, 1962; *DMSR*, Sept. 23, 1962; *CRG*, Nov. 1, 1962.

[32]By 1976, with the UAW comprising over 40,000 members, some 400 union workers would receive a full day's wages to work the precincts on election day; the money would come directly from state UAW funds. Interview with Edris "Soapy" Owens (Oct. 12, 1976, Newton, Iowa).

[33]*CRG*, Nov. 29, 1961, Aug. 14, 1962; Owens, interview (Oct. 12, 1976).

[34]*CRG*, Nov. 29, 1961; Owens, interview (Oct. 12, 1976).

NOTES

[35]Interview with Arthur Hedberg, Jr. (Oct. 7, 1976, Des Moines, Iowa); *DMR*, Feb. 25, 1962.

[36]A few years later, Ray would succeed Harold Hughes to become the youngest and longest-serving governor in Iowa history.

[37]*ICPC*, Dec. 10, 1963.

[38]*DMR*, Jan. 20, 1964.

[39]*DMR*, Dec. 8, 1963, Dec. 10, 1963; *CRG*, Dec. 10, 1963, June 17, 1964; *ICPC*, Dec. 16, 1963.

[40]*CRG*, Jan. 1, 1962.

[41]*Iowa Official Register*, 51 (1965-66) (Des Moines, Iowa, 1965), 398-495.

[42]*DMSR*, "The Iowa Poll," May 1, 1966; years 1967-75 from summary of "Iowa Poll" during that time period, provided to James Larew by the *Des Moines Register and Tribune*, April 4, 1977.

The data, by year:

	Republican	Democratic	Independent
1956	54	41	5
1957	51	43	6
1958	50	43	7
1959	48	41	11
1960	49	42	9
1961	47	40	13
1962	46	41	13
1963	47	36	17
1964	42	48	10
1965	42	52	6
1966	44	47	9
1967	45	47	8
1968	47	44	8
1969	46	47	7
1970	41	45	14
1971	45	44	10
1972	44	46	9
1973	42	44	14
1974	43	48	9
1975	42	46	12

[43]*Iowa Official Register*, (1965-66), pp. 399, 401, 409-10.

Hultman had joined Robert Ray at the state convention to support William Scranton for President. Hultman and Hughes varied very little on the issues, but the Republican made a crucial tactical blunder when he accused the Governor of having attempted, years earlier, to cover up a drunken-driving violation in the state of Florida. Hughes, who had been strikingly open about his problem with alcohol throughout his political career, responded: "If to win an election in Iowa you have to sneak, like a thief in the night through dark corridors, armed with poison darts and anonymous letters, I am not interested. We have had no fiery

NOTES
— 191 —

crosses burned, but perhaps that is scheduled for election eve." Public support rapidly swept to Hughes, and even Hultman's running mate for lieutenant governor, incumbent William L. Mooty, issued a statement that criticized Hultman and his handling of the issue. *DMTrib,* Oct. 31, 1964; *DMR,* Oct. 31, 1964, Nov. 1, 1963; *CRG,* Nov. 1, 1964.

[44] Frank T. Nye, "The 61st General Assembly of Iowa," *The Palimpsest,* 46 (Sept. 1965), 459; Ronald D. Hedlund and Charles W. Wiggins, "Legislative Politics in Iowa," in *Midwest Legislative Politics,* ed. Samuel Patterson (Iowa City, 1967), p. 22; *DMR,* Nov. 5, 1964.

[45] Nye, "The 61st General Assembly of Iowa," pp. 459-72.

[46] Donald A. Erickson, "Showdown at an Amish Schoolhouse," in *Compulsory Education and the Amish: The Right Not to be Modern,* ed. Albert N. Keim (Boston, 1975), pp. 43-45.

[47] *DMR,* Nov. 23, 1965.
[48] *DMR,* July 24, 1966.
[49] Erickson, pp. 43-72.
[50] *DMR,* Jan. 11, 1966; Erickson, p. 73.
[51] *DMR,* Jan. 11; 1966. Erickson, p. 73.
[52] *DMR,* Feb. 22, 1966.
[53] Erickson, p. 74.
[54] *DMR,* Feb. 23, 1966.
[55] *DMR,* Feb. 27, 1966.
[56] *DMR,* July 24, 1966.
[57] *DMR,* July 24, 1966.
[58] *DMR,* April 18, 1967.
[59] *DMR,* Dec. 30, 1964.
[60] *CRG,* Dec. 30, 1964; Jan. 29, 1965; Feb. 1, 1965.
[61] *DMR,* Feb. 17, 1965.
[62] Interview with Park Rinard (Sept. 14, 1976, Washington, D.C.).
[63] Interview with Robert Fulton (Dec. 8, 1976, Waterloo, Iowa).
[64] *CRG,* Feb. 1, 1965.
[65] *CRG,* Jan. 7, 1965.
[66] *CRG,* Jan. 29, 1965.
[67] *DMR,* March 9, 1965; *DMTrib,* March 9, 1965; *CRG,* April 20, 1965.
[68] Rinard, interview (Sept. 14, 1976).
[69] Nye, "The 61st General Assembly of Iowa," pp. 457-58. The Governor's special message called for consideration of three separate bills concerned with Iowa labor laws, designed to: (1) legalize union shop practices; (2) clarify statutes concerned with secondary boycotts, illegal labor practices such as "featherbedding," and the use of court injunctions in labor disputes; and (3) create a state mediation-conciliation board within the Iowa Bureau of Labor.
See also: *CRG,* May 5, 1965; *DMTrib,* May 5, 1965.

[70] *DMTrib,* April 17, 1965, May 22, 1965, May 24, 1965.
[71] Interview with Edris "Soapy" Owens (Oct. 12, 1976, Newton, Iowa); inter-

view with Hugh D. Clark, president of the Iowa AFL-CIO (Oct. 8, 1976, Des Moines, Iowa); *DMR,* June 20, 1966, Sept. 16, 1966.

[72]*DMR,* July 15, 1965.

[73]*DMTrib,* July 17, 1965.

[74]*DMR,* Sept. 11, 1965; *CRG,* Sept. 14, 1965. More also had received at least one-third of the vote.

[75]Interview with Clark Rasmussen (Oct. 13, 1976, Des Moines, Iowa).

[76]*DMR,* June 12, 1966.

[77]*DMR,* June 14, 1966.

[78]*CRG,* May 17, 1970. The endorsement provision of the Democratic state constitution was lifted by delegates to the 1970 Democratic state convention.

[79]*Iowa Official Register, 52* (1967-68) (Des Moines, Iowa, 1967), 47-67, 69-111; *DMR,* Nov. 10, 1966, Nov. 11, 1966; *ICPC,* Nov. 9, 1966.

[80]Interview with John C. Culver (Sept. 16, 1976, Washington, D.C.); *CRG,* Nov. 16, 1962; *DMTrib,* Nov. 9, 1966; *DMR,* Nov. 13, 1966.

[81]Larry L. King, "Harold E. Hughes: Evangelist From the Prairies," *Harpers,* March 1969, pp. 52-53.

[82]Nie, Verba, and Petrocik, p. 104.

[83]Frank T. Nye, "The 62nd General Assembly of Iowa," *The Palimpsest,* 48 (Nov. 1967), 528.

[84]Interview with James Flansburg (December 14, 1976, Des Moines, Iowa).

[85]John Herbers, "Democratic Candidates in Iowa Fear Effects of Nixon Coattails," *New York Times,* Oct. 28, 1968.

[86]*DMTrib,* Oct. 17, 1968, Nov. 6, 1968.

[87]*ICPC,* Aug. 2, 1969; *CRG,* May 17, 1970; Democratic Party of Iowa, "The Party Constitution of the Democratic Party of Iowa," (Article V, Section 3; Article VI, Section 2; Article VII, Sections 1 and 2), May 1, 1976.

[88]Don F. Hadwiger and Jim Hutter, "Party Orientation of Political Convention Delegates—1968, 1972, 1974" (paper presented to Midwest Political Science Meetings, Chicago, May 1975), p. 12.

[89]These changes in delegate memberships of Democratic conventions appear to have lagged behind more fundamental shifts in partisan preferences which began occurring in the early 1960s. Taking the 1952 election year as a base line (by 1956, a volatile farm vote awarded temporary successes to the Democratic Party) and using the Mather-Larew partisan preference ratings (that is, taking for each election year the arithmetic mean of the percent of the two-party vote cast Republican for president, senator, and governor in that election and the preceding two elections), one finds that the elections in the 1940s showed a closer correspondence (that is, votes compared on a county-to-county basis over time) to the 1952 election than those elections held in the late 1950s and early 1960s. By 1968 and 1970, it appears, the Iowa electorate had become—even if temporarily—less prone to realign than a decade earlier. The correlation coefficients, using 1952 as the baseline, are:

NOTES

1940	.741	1956	.937
1942	.863	1958	.890
1944	.911	1960	.870
1946	.928	1962	.847
1948	.953	1964	.836
1950	.985	1966	.806
1952	1.000	1968	.810
1954	.967	1970	.810

See: George B. Mather, *Effects of the Use of Voting Machines on Total Votes Cast: Iowa—1920 to 1960* (Iowa City, 1964), pp. 5-20 and update by author.

[90] Interview with David Stanley (Dec. 16, 1976, Muscatine, Iowa).

[91] Stanley, interview (Dec. 16, 1976); *DMR,* Nov. 3, 1968; Hughes and Schneider, p. 148.

[92] *DMSR,* Oct. 20, 1968.

[93] *Iowa Official Register,* 1965-66, p. 401; *Iowa Official Register,* 1969-70, p. 352; *Davenport Times-Democrat* (hereafter abbreviated *DavTD*), Sept. 26, 1968.

The *Des Moines Register* has played an important role in formulating issues in Iowa politics. The *Register* is of extremely high caliber (in 1976 only the *New York Times* had accumulated more Pulitzer Prizes over time than had the Des Moines paper) and has a statewide circulation that in 1977 reached six of every ten homes in the state. Generally speaking, its editorial policies have been more progressive than those of the state's citizens; it has been a leading early advocate of reapportionment, county government consolidation and reform, judicial reform, constitutional home rule for urban areas, private utility regulation, and many other critical issues including the anti-war posture taken in 1968 at about the same time that Harold Hughes changed his own views. In terms of political candidates, the *Register* has supported candidates of both parties. In 1968 it endorsed Richard Nixon, Harold Hughes, and Robert Ray; in 1972, Nixon, Dick Clark (Democrat for the U.S. Senate) and Ray were endorsed.

[94] *DavTD,* Nov. 10, 1968.

[95] Richard Bender and Ben Benzene, "The Computerized Statistics Collection Program of the Democratic Party of Iowa, 1966-1970," unpublished study by the Democratic Party of Iowa. The data:

	1966	1968	1970
Urban	63.7%	50.9%	50.5%
City	55.7	45.0	45.3
Town	50.6	40.7	43.2
Rural	51.7	45.0	48.9
Suburb	61.4	46.6	47.4
Farm	50.6	45.5	49.3

[96] Fulton, interview (Dec. 8, 1976).

[97] In 1967 the Iowa UAW split from the AFL-CIO, as had the national UAW. Always the most aggressively political group, the UAW was no longer encumbered by the less active unions. The split made a noticeable impact on Iowa Democratic politics. Before 1972, typically three or four delegates to national

NOTES

conventions had UAW ties. In 1972, the UAW sent six; by 1976, they claimed eleven of 47 delegates including the UAW head who also now served as the elected chief of the delegation. Iowa's UAW head, Chuck Gifford, who succeeded his father-in-law Soapy Owens to that position, increased that group's financial contributions to the state party.

Ben Benzene, paid political coordinator for the Iowa Democrats from 1971 to 1976 and former UAW shop steward from Waterloo, recalls: "In 1973, I raised $25,000 in labor contributions. Prior to my coming to the state party staff, labor put all their money into individual candidates. But, with my arrival, they agreed to contribute directly to the party. I can raise $30,000 to $40,000 a year from the labor unions alone." Interview with Ben Benzene (Dec. 9, 1976, Des Moines, Iowa).

— V —
THE ORGANIZED DEMOCRATS: JOHN CULVER, DICK CLARK, AND THE NEW PARTY MACHINERY

[1] Robert R. Dykstra and Russell M. Ross, "Toward Adjournment: The Second Session of the 65th General Assembly, 1973," *The Palimpsest,* 55 (November/December 1974), 184.

[2] Norman H. Nie, Sidney Verba, and John R. Petrocik, *The Changing American Voter* (Cambridge, Mass., 1976), pp. 49, 52. In 1966, Iowa's registration cities showed over 50% of the voters registered as Independents. By 1976, about 33% of all Iowa's voters would be registered Independents; 36% would be Democrats and about 31% would be Republicans.

[3] Interview with Mathew Wanning (Dec. 10, 1976, Des Moines, Iowa). Wanning, chief fundraiser for the Democratic Party from 1975 to 1976, provided the following list of money spent by the Democrats from 1966 to 1976:

1966	$141,000	1972	$214,800
1967	127,200	1973	171,600
1968	273,000	1974	220,085
1969	117,000	1975	209,780
1970	127,200	1976	263,711
1971	130,800		

[4] Interview with Edris "Soapy" Owens (Oct. 12, 1976, Newton, Iowa); interview with Hugh D. Clark (Oct. 8, 1976, Des Moines, Iowa). *Des Moines Register* (hereafter abbreviated *DMR*), April 9, 1965; *Des Moines Tribune* (hereafter abbreviated *DMTrib*), June 26, 1966.

[5] *DMR,* April 21, 1970, Sept. 29, 1972; *Cedar Rapids Gazette* (hereafter abbreviated *CRG*), June 14, 1971.

Since 1940, there has been an increasingly negative correlation between Republican vote and the degree of urbanization in counties. When Mather urbanism ratings for counties (that is, giving some weight to the factor of population density of counties rather than only total populations of those same coun-

NOTES
— 195 —

ties) are related to the Mather-Larew partisan preference ratings from 1940 to 1970, the following correlation coefficients are generated:

1940	−.12	1956	−.37
1942	−.16	1958	−.30
1944	−.28	1960	−.28
1946	−.27	1962	−.35
1948	−.29	1964	−.36
1950	−.27	1966	−.40
1952	−.38	1968	−.42
1954	−.43	1970	−.39

Source of correlations: George B. Mather, *Effects of the Use of Voting Machines on Total Votes Cast: Iowa—1920 to 1960.* Iowa City, 1964, p. 31; George B. Mather and James C. Larew, unpublished statistical update of *Effects of the Use of Voting Machines.*

Clearly, the Democratic Party has increasingly become the urban party. For Republicans to have placed new voter registration restrictions on the most populous counties directly discriminated against Democratic voters.

[6] Interview with Clark Rasmussen (Oct. 13, 1976, Des Moines, Iowa); interview with Tom Dawson (Sept. 15, 1976, Washington, D.C.).

[7] Interview with Ben Benzene (Dec. 9, 1976, Des Moines, Iowa).

[8] Benzene, interview (Dec. 9, 1976); *CRG,* Dec. 6, 1968.

[9] *DMR,* June 8, 1973; Benzene, interview (Dec. 9, 1976). To wipe out debts completely, close friends of Harold Hughes in 1973 and 1974 formed a committee to raise about $40,000 to pay off some of the $70,000 backlog, and other creditors were encouraged to forgive amounts owed to them.

[10] In 1938, Talle had been elected to the old Fourth District, many of whose counties were subsequently assigned to the Second Congressional District after the 1940 Census.

[11] Interview with Stephen B. Jackson (Sept. 10, 1979, Cedar Rapids, Iowa); interview with James R. Bromwell (July 24, 1979, Cedar Rapids, Iowa).

[12] Bromwell, interview (July 24, 1979).

[13] Bromwell, interview (July 24, 1979).

[14] *DMR,* Dec. 6, 1964.

[15] *DMR,* Dec. 6, 1964.

[16] Anne Taylor Fleming, "The Kennedy Mystique," *New York Times Sunday Magazine,* June 17, 1979, p. 18.

[17] Interview with John C. Culver (Sept. 16, 1976, Washington, D.C.).

[18] Interview with Teri Ferguson (Sept. 11, 1979, Cedar Rapids, Iowa).

[19] Interview with Dick Clark (Sept. 28, 1979, Washington, D.C.).

[20] *CRG,* Nov. 8, 1964.

[21] Culver, interview (Sept. 16, 1976).

[22] *DMR,* Dec. 6, 1964.

[23] Culver, interview (Sept. 16, 1976).

[24] *CRG,* Oct. 26, 1964; Culver, interview (Sept. 16, 1976); Ferguson, interview (Sept. 11, 1979).

NOTES

[25] *CRG,* Nov. 4, 1964.
[26] *Dubuque Telegraph-Herald,* Oct. 23, 1964.
[27] Culver, interview (Sept. 16, 1976).
[28] Jackson, interview (Sept. 10, 1979); Ferguson, interview (Sept. 11, 1979).
[29] Dick Clark, interview (Sept. 28, 1979).
[30] *CRG,* Nov. 8, 1964.
[31] Dick Clark, interview (Sept. 28, 1979).
[32] *Clinton Herald,* Oct. 17, 1964.
[33] *Cascade Pioneer-Advertiser,* June 25, 1964.
[34] *West Union Fayette County Union and West Union Argo-Gazette,* Aug. 13, 1964.
[35] *DMR,* Dec. 6, 1964.
[36] *DMR,* Dec. 6, 1964.
[37] *DMR,* Oct. 4, 1964, Dec. 6, 1964.
[38] *CRG,* Sept. 8, 1964.
[39] *Cedar Rapids Citizen Times,* Aug. 30, 1964.
[40] *Ossian Bee,* June 18, 1964.
[41] *DMR,* Dec. 6, 1964.
[42] Culver, interview (Sept. 16, 1976).
[43] Culver, interview (Sept. 16, 1976).
[44] *Decorah Journal,* July 23, 1964.
[45] *Iowa Official Register,* 1965-66, pp. 432-41.
[46] *CRG,* Nov. 11, 1966.
[47] Bromwell, interview (July 24, 1979).
[48] *CRG,* Sept. 10, 1966.
[49] Ferguson, interview (Sept. 11, 1979).
[50] *Oelwein Daily Register,* Dec. 9, 1965.
[51] *DeWitt Observer,* April 22, 1965; *McGregor North Iowa Times,* Sept. 2, 1965; *Clinton Herald,* May 3, 1965.
[52] *CRG,* Nov. 2, 1966.
[53] *CRG,* Oct. 2, 1966; *DMR,* Oct. 28, 1965.
[54] *DMR,* Oct. 28, 1965; *Dubuque Telegraph-Herald,* Sept. 25, 1966.
[55] *Maquoketa Jackson Sentinel,* Nov. 3, 1966.
[56] *DeWitt Observer,* Nov. 1, 1966.
[57] *CRG,* Oct. 3, 1966.
[58] *CRG,* Oct. 30, 1966.
[59] *Dubuque Telegraph-Herald,* Oct. 10, 1966.
[60] *CRG,* Oct. 26, 1966, Oct. 30, 1966.
[61] Dick Clark, interview (Sept. 28, 1979).
[62] Jackson, interview (Sept. 10, 1979).
[63] Dick Clark, interview (Sept. 10, 1979).
[64] Dick Clark, interview (Sept. 10, 1979).
[65] *DMR,* Oct. 10, 1968.
[66] *DMR,* Oct. 23, 1968.

NOTES
— 197 —

[67]*CRG*, Oct. 27, 1968.
[68]*CRG*, Jan. 15, 1968; *DMR*, Oct. 25, 1968.
[69]Dick Clark, interview (Sept. 10, 1979).
[70]*ICPC*, Oct. 30, 1970.
[71]*CRG*, Oct. 28, 1970.
[72]*DMR*, Oct. 23, 1970.
[73]Culver, interview (Sept. 16, 1976).
[74]*Davenport Times-Democrat* (hereafter abbreviated *DavTD*), Feb. 11, 1972.
[75]Interview with Bob Miller (Sept. 21, 1979, Washington, D.C.); interview with Andy Loewi (Sept. 18, 1979, Boston, Mass.).
[76]*DavTD*, Feb. 11, 1972.
[77]Dick Clark, interview (Sept. 10, 1979).
[78]Dick Clark, interview (Sept. 10, 1979).
[79]*DavTD*, Nov. 1, 1972.
[80]*DavTD*, Mar. 24, 1974; interview with Cliff Larson (Oct. 13, 1976, Ames, Iowa).
[81]Interview with Robert D. Ray (Dec. 22, 1976, Des Moines, Iowa).
[82]Note, for example, the general upward trend in the proportion of the electorate voting for Democratic candidates in congressional races in the Second District and in the State of Iowa during the period 1950-1974.

Congressional Vote, 1950-1974
Percentage Voting Democratic

Year	Second District	State of Iowa
1950	41.2%	38.2%
1952	37.7	32.3
1954	44.6	41.2
1956	48.6	45.0
1958	51.1	50.1
1960	47.5	45.6
1962	47.2	42.7
1964	52.2	55.0
1966	54.0	46.3
1968	55.1	43.8
1970	60.5	47.5
1972	59.2	50.2
1974	51.5	54.7

Source: *Iowa Official Register*, 1949-1950 to 1975-1976.

BIBLIOGRAPHY

BOOKS

Andrews, Clarence A. *A Literary History of Iowa.* Iowa City: Univ. of Iowa Press, 1972.

Block, William J. *The Separation of the Farm Bureau and the Extension Service: Political Issues in a Federal System.* Urbana: Univ. of Illinois Press, 1960.

Cochrane, Willard W., and Mary E. Ryan. *American Farm Policy, 1948-1973.* Minneapolis: Univ. of Minnesota Press, 1976.

David, Paul T. *Party Strength in the United States, 1872-1970.* Charlottesville: Univ. Press of Virginia, 1972.

Devries, Walter, and Lance Tarrance, Jr. *The Ticket Splitter: A New Force in American Politics.* Grand Rapids, Mich.: William B. Eerdman, 1972.

Erbe, William. *Urbanization, Migration and Social Change: Iowa Enters the 1970's.* Iowa City: Iowa Urban Community Research Center, 1973.

Fenton, John H. *Midwest Politics.* New York: Holt, Rinehart and Winston, 1966.

Foner, Eric. *Free Soil, Free Labor, Free Men: The Ideology of the Republican Party Before the Civil War.* New York: Oxford Univ. Press, 1970.

Hahn, Harlan. *Urban-Rural Conflict: The Politics of Change.* Beverly Hills, Calif.: Sage Press, 1971.

Haynes, Fred E. *Third Party Movements Since the Civil War: With Special Reference to Iowa.* Iowa City: State Historical Society of Iowa, 1916.

Hofstadter, Richard. *The American Political Tradition: And the Men Who Made It.* New York: Alfred A. Knopf, 1948.

Hofstadter, Richard, William Miller, and Daniel Aaron. *The United States: The History of a Republic.* 2nd ed. Englewood Cliffs, N.J.: Prentice-Hall, 1957.

Hoover, Herbert. *The Memoirs of Herbert Hoover.* Vols. I and II. New York: Macmillan, 1951.

Hughes, Harold E., and Dick Schneider. *The Man from Ida Grove: A Senator's Personal Story.* Lincoln, Va.: Chosen Books, 1979.

Hull, John A.T. *Census of Iowa for 1880 (1836-1880).* Des Moines: F.M. Mills, 1883.

Iowa Agricultural Experiment Station. *A Century of Farming in Iowa, 1846-1946.* Ames: Iowa State College Press, 1946.

Iowa Federation of Labor, AFL-CIO. *Proceedings of the Annual Convention of the Iowa Federation of Labor, AFL-CIO, June 27-28, 1956.* Des Moines: Iowa Federation of Labor, 1956.

Iowa Official Register, 1955-56 to 1969-70.

BIBLIOGRAPHY

Jensen, Richard. *The Winning of the Midwest: Social and Political Conflict, 1888-1896.* Chicago: Univ. of Chicago Press, 1971.

Kantor, MacKinlay. *But Look the Morn: The Story of a Childhood.* London: Falcon Press, 1950.

Kellogg, Dennis, and Charles W. Wiggins. *Party Voting in the Sixty-Fifth General Assembly.* Ames: Dept. of Political Science, Iowa State Univ., 1974.

LaFollette, Robert M. *LaFollette's Autobiography: A Personal Narrative of Political Experiences.* Madison: The Robert M. LaFollette Company, 1913.

Lubell, Samuel. *The Future of American Politics.* 3rd ed. New York: Harper Colophon Books, Harper and Row, 1965.

Mather, George B. *Effects of the Use of Voting Machines on Total Votes Cast: Iowa—1920 to 1960.* Iowa City: Institute of Public Affairs, Univ. of Iowa, 1964.

Miller, Merle. *Plain Speaking: An Oral Biography of Harry S. Truman.* New York: Putnam, 1973.

Nie, Norman H., Sidney Verba, and John R. Petrocik. *The Changing American Voter.* Cambridge: Harvard Univ. Press, 1976.

Nye, Russell B. *Midwestern Progressive Politics: A Historical Study of Its Origins and Developments, 1870-1950.* East Lansing: Michigan State College Press, 1951.

Peirce, Neal R. *The Great Plains States: People, Politics, and Power in the Nine Great Plains States.* New York: Norton, 1972.

Pelzer, Louis. *The Origin and Organization of the Republican Party in Iowa.* Iowa City: State Historical Society of Iowa, 1907.

Powers, Ronald C., and Sue Meyers. *The Population Change of the Fort Dodge Area.* Ames: Iowa State Univ. Extension Service Bulletin No. 335, 1966.

Prior, Jean Cutler. *A Regional Guide to Iowa Landforms.* Iowa City: Iowa Geological Survey, 1976.

Rehmus, Charles M., and Doris B. McLaughlin. *Labor and American Politics: A Book of Readings.* Ann Arbor: Univ. of Michigan Press, 1967.

Rogin, Michael Paul. *The Intellectuals and McCarthy: The Radical Specter.* Cambridge, Mass.: M.I.T. Press, 1967.

Rosenberg, Morton Mervin. *Iowa on the Eve of the Civil War: A Decade of Frontier Politics.* Norman,: Univ. of Oklahoma Press, 1972.

Ross, Thomas Richard. *Jonathan Prentiss Dolliver: A Study in Political Integrity and Independence.* Iowa City: State Historical Society of Iowa, 1958.

Sage, Leland L. *A History of Iowa.* Ames: Iowa State Univ. Press, 1974.

———. *William Boyd Allison: A Study in Practical Politics.* Iowa City: State Historical Society of Iowa, 1956.

Salisbury, Neil Elloit, and Gerald Rushton. *Growth and Decline of Iowa Villages: A Pilot Study.* Iowa City: Dept. of Geography, Univ. of Iowa, 1963.

Scammon, Richard M. *America Votes 10: A Handbook of Contemporary American Election Statistics.* Washington, D.C.: Government Affairs Institute, 1973.

BIBLIOGRAPHY

Schmidhauser, John R. *Iowa's Campaign for a Constitutional Convention in 1960.* New York: McGraw-Hill, 1963.
Shambaugh, Benjamin F. *History of the Constitutions of Iowa.* Des Moines: Historical Department of Iowa, 1902.
Suckow, Ruth. *Some Others and Myself: Seven Stories and a Memoir.* New York: Rinehart, 1932.
Sundquist, James L. *Dynamics of the Party System: Alignment and Realignment of Political Parties in the United States.* Washington, D.C.: Brookings Institution, 1973.
Tait, John L., and Arthur H. Johnson. *Iowa Population Trends.* Ames: Iowa State Univ. Press, 1971.
Throne, Mildred. *Cyrus Clay Carpenter and Iowa Politics, 1854-1898.* Iowa City: State Historical Society of Iowa, 1974.
University of Iowa, Institute of Public Affairs. *Facts and Opinions about the Shaff Plan.* Iowa City: Univ. of Iowa, 1963.
U.S. Dept. of Commerce, Bureau of Census. *Seventeenth Census of the United States: Population, 1950.* Vol. 2, part 1. Washington, D.C.: GPO, 1952.
_____. *Eighteenth Census of the United States: Population, 1960.* Vol. 1, part 14. Washington, D.C.: GPO, 1962.
_____. *Nineteenth Census of the United States: Population, 1970.* Vol. 1, part 17. Washington, D.C.: GPO, 1973.
_____. *Historical Statistics of the United States: Colonial Times to 1970.* Part I. Washington, D.C.: GPO, 1975.
_____. *Statistical Abstract of the United States: 1978.* Washington, D.C.: GPO, 1978.
U.S. House of Representatives. *Statutes at Large.* Volume XXXVIII. Washington, D.C.: GPO, 1914.
Wall, Joseph Frazier. *Iowa: A Bicentennial History.* New York: W.W. Norton, 1978.

Articles

"Band of Brothers." *Newsweek,* June 17, 1974, p. 72.
Bonjean, Charles M., and Robert L. Lineberry. "Urbanization-Party Competition Hypothesis: A Comparison of All United States Counties." *Journal of Politics,* 32 (May 1970), 305-21.
Bourjaily, Vance. "The Governor from Ida Grove." *New York Times Magazine,* Feb. 26, 1967, pp. 34-35.
Buerer, Jerrold L. "Urbanization and Political Party Competition in the State of Iowa." *Urbanization, Migration and Social Changes: Iowa Enters the 1970's,* pp. 55-66. Ed. William Erbe. Iowa City: Iowa Urban Community Research Center, 1973.
Deakin, James. "1972? Well let's see now . . . and then there's Harold. Harold?" *Esquire,* Feb. 1970, pp. 55, 139-41.
"Democrats: The Dark Horse." *Newsweek,* March 2, 1970, pp. 30-31.

BIBLIOGRAPHY

Dykstra, Robert. "Iowa: Bright Radical Star." *Radical Republicans in the North: State Politics During Reconstruction,* pp. 167-93. Ed. James C. Mohr. Baltimore: Johns Hopkins Univ. Press, 1976.

Dykstra, Robert, and Russell M. Ross. "Toward Adjournment: The Second Session of the 65th General Assembly, 1973." *The Palimpsest,* 55 (November/December 1974), 184-89.

"Elections: The Fourth Dimension." *Time,* Dec. 28, 1959, p. 11.

Erickson, Donald A. "Showdown at an Amish Schoolhouse." *Compulsory Education and the Amish: The Right Not To Be Modern,* pp. 43-83. Ed. Albert N. Keim. Boston: Beacon Press, 1975.

Fleming, Anne Taylor. "The Kennedy Mystique." *New York Times Sunday Magazine,* June 17, 1979, pp. 14-24, 44-48.

"Forty-two States Reapportion: Plans are 'Final' in Twenty-one." *American Legislator,* May 1972, p. 2.

Gold, David, and John R. Schmidhauser. "Urbanization and Party Competition: The Case of Iowa." *Midwest Journal of Political Science,* 4 (1960), 63-65.

Hedlund, Ronald D., and Charles W. Wiggins. "Legislative Politics in Iowa." *Midwest Legislative Politics,* pp. 7-36. Ed. Samuel Patterson. Iowa City: Institute of Public Affairs, Univ. of Iowa, 1967.

Key, V. O., Jr. "A Theory of Critical Elections." *Journal of Politics,* 17 (February 1955), 3-18.

King, Larry L. "Harold E. Hughes: Evangelist from the Prairies." *Harpers,* March 1969, pp. 50-57.

May, George S. "Recent Industrial Development." *The Palimpsest,* 37 (May 1956), 229-32.

Melhorn, Donna J. "Representation in the General Assembly." *Iowa Business Digest,* 31 (August 1960), 16-19.

Nordquist, Gerald L. "A Summary of Economic and Social Developments in Iowa." *Iowa Business Digest,* 31 (August 1960), 4-9.

Northam, Ray M. "Declining Urban Centers in the United States: 1940-1960." *Annals of the Association of American Geographers,* 53 (March 1963), 50-59.

Nye, Frank T. "Reapportionment in Iowa." *The Palimpsest,* 45 (June 1964), 241-72.

_____. "The 60th General Assembly of Iowa." *The Palimpsest,* 44 (Oct. 1963), 444-49.

_____. "The 61st General Assembly of Iowa." *The Palimpsest,* 46 (Sept. 1965), 425-88.

_____. "The 62nd General Assembly of Iowa." *The Palimpsest,* 48 (Nov. 1967), 505-08.

"One for O'Brien." *New Republic,* Oct. 23, 1971, pp. 9-10.

"Over the Anthills." *Time,* Oct. 22, 1956, pp. 24-26.

Roll, Charles. "Political Trends in Iowa History." *Iowa Journal of History and Politics,* 26 (Oct. 1928), 449-519.

BIBLIOGRAPHY

Rumage, Kennard W. "Some Spatial Characteristics of the Republican and Democratic Vote in Iowa, 1900-1956." *Iowa Business Digest, 31* (Winter 1960), 17-21.

Russell, J.S. "Iowa's Farm-to-City Shift Is Speeding Up." *Iowa Farm and Home Register,* supplement to *Des Moines Sunday Register,* May 15, 1960, p. 5-H.

Sparks, David S. "The Decline of the Democratic Party in Iowa, 1850-1860." *Iowa Journal of History,* 53 (Jan. 1955), 1-30.

Thimmesch, Nick. "The Lord and Harold Hughes." *Saturday Evening Post,* June/July 1974, pp. 42-45.

Wall, James M. "A Senator's Faith and Vocation." *Christian Century,* Sept. 26, 1973, pp. 931-32.

Wieck, Paul R. "Hard-Pressed Democrats in Iowa." *New Republic,* Oct. 19, 1968, pp. 13-15.

____. "The Presidential Candidacy of Harold Hughes: For God and Country." *New Republic,* May 15, 1971, pp. 19-24.

Wiggins, Charles W. "Constitutional Convention Issue in Iowa, 1960." *Annals of Iowa,* 3rd. series, 40 (Winter 1970), 171-90.

____. "The Post World War II Legislative Reapportionment Battle in Iowa Politics." *Patterns and Perspectives in Iowa History,* pp. 403-30. Ed. Dorothy Schwieder. Ames: Iowa State Univ. Press, 1973.

Unpublished Material

Bender, Richard, and Ben Benzene. "The Computerized Statistics Collection Program of the Democratic Party of Iowa, 1966-1970." State Democratic Headquarters, Des Moines, Iowa.

Billman, John Irwin. "Early Iowa, the Genesis of a Western State." Written for the Veterans of Foreign Wars of the United States, 1931. State Historical Society, Iowa City, Iowa.

Culver, John Chester. "Legislative Apportionment: The Iowa Story." B.A. honors thesis, Harvard University, 1954.

Democratic Party of Iowa. "The Party Constitution of the Democratic Party of Iowa." Ratified May 1, 1976. State Democratic Headquarters, Des Moines, Iowa.

____. "Targetting Information for the 1976 Campaign." Election statistics compiled by the Democratic Party of Iowa, Des Moines. State Democratic Headquarters, Des Moines, Iowa.

Erickson, Erling Arthur. "Banks and Politics Before the Civil War: The Case of Iowa, 1836-1865." Ph.D. dissertation, University of Iowa, 1967.

Full, Merle Fleming. "Until Hell Freezes Over." An analysis of Harold E. Hughes as governor of Iowa, 1968.

Garst, Roswell. "Corn History and History of Nitrogen Usage and Corn Production Utilizing 5-year Averages from 1930-1974, compiled from USDA Figures," Oct. 22, 1974. Author's copy.

BIBLIOGRAPHY

Gibson, James Richard. "Party Organization: A Conceptual Analysis of a Campaign in Iowa." M.A. thesis, University of Iowa, 1972.
Hahn, Harlan Dean. "One-Partyism and State Politics: The Structure of Political Power in Iowa." Ph.D. dissertation, Harvard University, 1964.
Hadwiger, Donald F., and James L. Hutter. "Party Orientation of Political Convention Delegates—1968, 1972, 1974." Midwest Political Science Meetings, Chicago, May 1975.
Hutter, James L., and Donald F. Hadwiger. "Characteristics of Lower-Level Party Leaders: Delegates to the Iowa Party Conventions." American Political Science Assn., Annual Meeting, San Francisco, Sept. 1975.
Iowa Development Commission. "Demographic and Economic Statistics, Summary." 1972. Government Documents, University of Iowa Library.
Kulisheck, Robert J. "Political Activism at the Grassroots: Study of County Organizations in Iowa." Ph. D. dissertation, University of Iowa, 1972.
Mather, George B., and James C. Larew. Statistical update of *Effects of the Use of Voting Machines on Total Votes Cast: Iowa—1920 to 1960.* [Iowa City: Institute of Public Affairs, University of Iowa, 1964] January 1977.
Nelson, Phyllis Ann. "George D. Herron and the Socialist Clergy, 1890-1914." Ph.D. dissertation, University of Iowa, 1953.
Rosenberg, Morton M. "The Democratic Party of Iowa, 1850-1860." Ph.D. dissertation, University of Iowa, 1957.
Ryan, Thomas G. "The Early Years of the Iowa Democratic Revival, 1950-1956." Conference of Iowa College Teachers of History, Cedar Falls, Iowa, Oct. 14, 1978.
Schou, John Thomas. "The Decline of the Democratic Party in Iowa, 1916-1920." M.A. thesis, University of Iowa, 1960.
Thomas, David L. "An Explanatory Model for City Size and Growth." M.A. thesis, University of Iowa, 1960.
Throne, Mildred A. "A History of Agriculture in Southern Iowa, 1833-1890." Ph.D. dissertation, University of Iowa, 1946.
Ungs, Thomas D. "The Republican Party in Iowa, 1946-1956." Ph.D. dissertation, University of Iowa, 1957.
Weiskind, Stewart L. "Settlement Changes and Spatial Behavior in Iowa: 1930-1960." M.A. thesis, Ohio State University, 1969.
Wells, Richard S. "The Legal Profession and Political Ideology—The Case of the Carr Law Firm of Manchester, Iowa." Ph.D. dissertation, University of Iowa, 1963.
Wiggins, Charles W. "Interest Group Power Within State Legislative Systems: The Case of the Iowa Farm Bureau Federation." Ph.D. dissertation, Washington University of St. Louis, 1964.

Manuscript Collections

Herschel Loveless Papers, Governor of Iowa, 1953-1961. Special Collections Department, University of Iowa Libraries, Iowa City, Iowa.

BIBLIOGRAPHY

Donald J. Mitchell Papers, Democratic National Committeeman from Iowa, 1963-1968. Special Collections Department, University of Iowa Libraries, Iowa City, Iowa.

Donald C. Pierson Papers, Chairman of the Iowa Republican State Central Committee, 1954-1957. Special Collections Department, University of Iowa Libraries, Iowa City, Iowa.

Newspapers

Cascade Pioneer-Advertiser, Feb. 18, 1966.
Cedar Rapids Gazette, 1948-74.
Clinton Herald, 1964-65.
Council Bluffs Nonpareil, Nov. 8, 1950.
Davenport Times-Democrat, 1960-74.
Decorah Journal, July 23, 1964.
Des Moines Register, 1948-74.
Des Moines Sunday Register, 1948-74.
Des Moines Tribune, 1948-70.
DeWitt Observer, 1965-66.
Dubuque Telegraph-Herald, 1964-66.
Iowa City Press-Citizen, 1950-70.
Maquoketa Jackson Sentinel, Nov. 3, 1966.
McGregor North Iowa Times, Sept. 2, 1965.
New York Times, Oct. 28, 1968.
Oelwein Daily Register, Dec. 9, 1965.
Omaha World-Herald, Oct. 16, 1957.
Ossian Bee, June 18, 1964.
West Union Fayette County Union and West Union Argo-Gazette, Aug. 13, 1964.

Interviews

George Anthan. Sept. 16, 1976. Washington, D.C.
Richard Bender. Sept. 12, 1976. Washington, D.C.
Benjamin Benzene. Dec. 9, 1976. Des Moines, Iowa.
James R. Bromwell. July 24, 1979. Cedar Rapids, Iowa.
Edward Campbell. Oct. 7, 1976. Des Moines, Iowa.
John Chrystal. Oct. 15, 1976. Coon Rapids, Iowa.
Dick Clark. Sept. 28, 1979. Washington, D.C.
Hugh D. Clark. Oct. 8, 1976. Des Moines, Iowa.
Wade P. Clarke. Oct. 14, 1976. Des Moines, Iowa.
John C. Culver. Sept. 16, 1976. Washington, D.C.
Thomas Dawson. Sept. 15, 1976. Washington, D.C.
Michael Doyle. Oct. 13, 1976. Des Moines, Iowa.
Teri Ferguson. Sept. 11, 1979. Cedar Rapids, Iowa.
James Flansburg. Dec. 14, 1976. Des Moines, Iowa.

BIBLIOGRAPHY
— 206 —

Robert Fulton. Dec. 8, 1976. Waterloo, Iowa.
Roswell Garst. Oct. 15, 1976. Coon Rapids, Iowa.
Dick Gilbert. Dec. 15, 1976. Des Moines, Iowa.
Tom Harkin. Sept. 16, 1976. Washington, D.C.
Arthur Hedberg, Jr. Oct. 7, 1976. Des Moines, Iowa.
Stephen B. Jackson. Sept. 10, 1979. Cedar Rapids, Iowa.
Robert L. Johnston. Jan. 6, 1976. Chicago, Illinois.
Cliff Larson. Oct. 13, 1976. Ames, Iowa.
Andy Loewi. Sept. 18, 1979. Cambridge, Massachusetts.
Herschel Loveless. Sept. 15, 1976. Washington, D.C.
Bob Miller. Sept. 21, 1979. Washington, D.C.
Jack Miller. Sept. 12, 1976. Washington, D.C.
George M. Mills. Dec. 14, 1976. Des Moines, Iowa.
Jake More. Oct. 8, 1976. Des Moines, Iowa.
Donald R. "Duke" Norbert. Sept. 16, 1976. Washington, D.C.
Frank T. Nye. Aug. 10, 1976. Cedar Rapids, Iowa.
Edris "Soapy" Owens. Oct. 12, 1976. Newton, Iowa.
Clark Rasmussen. Oct. 13, 1976. Des Moines, Iowa.
Robert D. Ray. Dec. 22, 1976. Des Moines, Iowa.
Park Rinard. Sept. 14, 1976. Washington, D.C.
James Risser. Sept. 16, 1976. Washington, D.C.
Joseph Rosenfield. Dec. 14, 1976. Des Moines, Iowa.
James Sarcone. Oct. 13, 1976. Des Moines, Iowa.
Fred Schwengel. Aug. 18, 1976. Kansas City, Missouri.
E.B. Smith. Sept. 21, 1976. College Park, Maryland.
Neal Smith. Sept. 16, 1976. Washington, D.C.
David M. Stanley. Dec. 16, 1976. Muscatine, Iowa.
Kenneth Thatcher. Oct. 4, 1976. Cummins, Iowa.
Mathew Wanning. Dec. 10, 1976. Des Moines, Iowa.

INDEX

AFL-CIO, Iowa: merger (1956), 19-20, 53; political platform of 1956, 54.
Agnew, Spiro T., 167.
Agrarian radicalism, 3-7.
Agriculture, Iowa, and export commodities, 7; grain prices, 4; land tax credits, 95; price support proposals, 56-57; productivity, 26.
Albia, 60, 62.
Alcoholism, 119.
Aldrich, Nelson W., 6.
Allamakee County, 135-136, 146.
Allison, William Boyd, 6.
Ames, 61, 87, 108.
Amish education controversy of 1965, 96f.
Anamosa, 142.
Anti-Monopoly Party, 3, 4.
Anti-union sentiment, 11, 17.
Associated General Contractors of Iowa, 20.
Associated Milk Producers, Inc., 171.

Beardsley, William, 12, 47-48, 50.
Beck, Robert, 108.
Beier, Fred, 97.
Benson, Ezra Taft, 18, 56-57.
Benton County, 135-36.
Billboards, 119.
Bingo, legalization of, 95.
Blue, Robert D., 32.
Boies, Horace, 5.
Borntreger, Dan, 104.

Borntreger, Emanuel, 97.
Bourjaily, Vance, 82.
Branch registration sites, 130.
Bromwell, James R., 137, 141-42, 145-46, 150-51, 154-55, 157, 159-60, 164; campaign of 1964, 145, 154; legislative record, 138.
Brookhart, Smith W., 6-7.
Bryan, William Jennings, 5.
Buchanan County, 135.

Campaign financing, 128.
Campaign practices, see Democratic Party of Iowa.
Campbell, Edward, 81.
Candidate preferences, 129.
Capital gains tax, 56.
Capital punishment, 95, 119.
Cascade, 142.
Cascade *Pioneer-Advertiser,* 150.
Cedar Rapids, 135-39, 142, 146-49, 153, 157, 161, 167.
Cedar Rapids *Gazette,* 59, 66, 89.
Cheap money, 4.
Cigarette tax, 56, 95.
Civil Service, 13; reforms, 128.
Civil War, 1-3, 8, 32, 54, 74, 127, 146.
Clark, Richard C., 9; campaign techniques, 74, 143; role in Culver campaigns, 2, 132-33, 141, 144-45, 147, 157, 162, 168; political background, 144; U.S. Senate campaign of 1972, 133-34, 169-70; walking tour of Iowa (1972), 169-70.

INDEX

Clarke, Wade P., 37-38, 40, 42, 59.
Clarinda State Mental Hospital, 39.
Clayton County, 135.
Clinton, 53, 66, 136, 146-49.
Clinton County, 135-36, 149, 163, 166.
Closed shop agreements, *see* Labor laws.
Coad, Merwin, 87-88.
Collins Radio Company, 135.
Commission on Economic and Social Trends in Iowa ("Committee of One Hundred"), 59.
Commodity prices, 56.
Community colleges, 95.
Computerized voter identification system, 74, 168, 173. *See also* Democratic Party of Iowa.
Congress of Industrial Organizations (CIO), 11, 19-20, 52.
Congressional elections, *see* Elections.
Consumer consciousness, 27.
Consumer protection law, 119.
Constitutional convention, proposed (1960), 67-70.
Coolidge, Calvin, 7.
Copperhead Democrats, 3.
Corporation tax, 56.
Couch, A. A., 53.
Coughlin, Father Charles E., 7.
Council Bluffs, 107.
County agents, 17.
County government costs, 30.
County party meetings, 19.
Culver, Ann, 149, 158.
Culver, John C., 2, 9, 118, 132-33, 140; achievements of first congressional term, 159; campaign techniques, 74, 141-42; catalog of supporters, 143; and community development projects, 157; congressional campaign of 1964, 92, 118, 141, 145-48, 154-55; congressional campaign of 1966, 117-18, 162; congressional campaign of 1968, 123, 163-65; and constituent service, 157-60; "Culver coordinators" (1964), 145; enlists Richard C. Clark as campaign manager (1963), 143-44; decides not to run for U.S. Senate in 1972, 133, 169; and the Kennedy family, 149, 161; leads congressional tours through the Second District, 157-58; legislative aims 1964-65, 157; personal background, 147-50; political background, 147-50; political philosophy, 151; political style, 118, 149-50; Senate campaign of 1974, 127-28, 134, 172.
Culver, Kay, 149.
Cummins, Albert Baird, 6.

Danforth Foundation, 104.
Davenport, 15.
Davis, Vern L., 111.
Dawson, Tom, 88.
Daylight savings time, 95.
Decorah, 136.
Delaware County, 135.
Democratic National Convention of 1968, 120-22.
Democratic Party of Iowa, 1, 7, 8; canvassing program (1952), 40-42; Central Committee, 42, 90,

INDEX

148; changes in membership (1968-1972), 74, 122; coalition with labor unions, 46, 51-54; county central committees, 42, 148; fund-raising efforts 1966-1974, 131; grass-roots organization, 9, 89-90; and Governor Harold E. Hughes, 8, 71, 73, 78, 119; internal revolt of 1954, 45-46; and labor laws, 54, 110-16; losses in 1972 election, 171; new party machinery of the 1970s, 74, 134; organizational techniques, 2, 40-43, 74, 143f, 168f, 173; Polk County organization, 39-40; state chair, 71, 74; state convention of 1958, 59-61; state convention of 1964, 110-16; strength of organization in 1940s, 2, 12; strength of organization in 1970s, 9, 74; support for income tax check-off law, 132; voter registration efforts of 1952, 41-42.
Depression (1930s), 1, 7, 16.
Des Moines, 2, 8, 37, 40-41, 43, 49, 82, 105, 115, 120, 127, 129.
Des Moines City Council, 42.
Des Moines Register, 23, 33, 66, 77, 85, 107, 123, 144.
Des Moines River, 54, 82.
DeWitt *Observer,* 160.
Dexter, 15.
Direct primary, 6.
Dolliver, Jonathan P., 6.
Domino theory (Southeast Asia), 164.
Domsalla, Harold, 149.
Dormitory towns, 25.
Doyle, Michael, 41.

Dubuque, 136, 146-49, 158.
Dubuque County, 135-36, 163.

Eisenhower, Dwight D., 48, 52, 54, 56, 63, 78, 137.
Elections: Congressional, of 1950, 46; of 1952, 48; of 1958, 63, 137; of 1960, 69-70, 137; of 1962, 87, 138; of 1964, 92, 155; of 1966, 116, 163; of 1968, 123, 165; of 1970, 167; of 1972, 171; of 1974, 127, 175.
 General, 46, 67, 90, 116-17.
 Gubernatorial, of 1950, 46; of 1952, 48; of 1954, 49-50; of 1956, 54, 58, 74-75; of 1958, 12, 63; of 1960, 67-68; of 1962, 77, 87; of 1964, 92; of 1966, 117; of 1968, 123.
 in Polk County, 38-39, 43-45.
 Senatorial, of 1950, 46; of 1956, 54; of 1960, 68-69; of 1962, 87, 89; of 1966, 116; of 1968, 123-24; of 1972, 170; of 1974, 127-28, 175.
Election laws, 130, 131.
Elkader, 75, 137.
Elvers, Adolph, 75.
Erbe, Norman, 68, 74-77.
Extension Service (USDA), 17-18.

Farm Bureau Federation, *see:* Iowa Farm Bureau Federation.
Farmers' Holiday Association, 7.
Fayette, 143-44.
Fayette County, 135-36, 153.
Fayette County *Union,* 105, 150.
Federal projects, 161.
Federal Renegotiation Board, 70.
Feld, James E., 145, 154.

INDEX

Ferguson, Teri, 142.
Flansburg, James (*Des Moines Register*), 123.
Food and drug laws, 6.
Ford, Gerald, 161.
Franzenburg, Paul, 123.
Freeman, Orville, 70.
Fulton, Robert D., 65, 94; 1970 gubernatorial candidacy, 124-25.
Funding of political candidates, 128.

Garst, Roswell, 23.
Gasoline tax, 56, 95.
General Assembly, see Iowa, General Assembly.
Ghettos, 126.
Gillette, Sen. Guy M., 7, 15.
Goldwater, Barry, 78, 91, 116, 151, 153, 155.
Governor's Reapportionment Action Committee, 59.
Grain elevator companies, 6.
Grange (Patrons of Husbandry), 3, 4.
Grassley, Charles, 175.
Great Depression, 1, 7, 16.
Great Society (Johnson Administration social programs), 95.
Greenbackers, 3-5.
Gregerson, Mary Pat, 107.
Gross, H. R., 92.
Gubernatorial elections, see elections.
Gun control legislation, 82, 122.
Guttenburg, 158.

Harper's magazine, 7.
Harris, Louis, 69.

Harvard College, John C. Culver at, 138-39.
Haugen, Gilbert, 7.
Hawarden, 28.
Hawkins, Lex, 40, 42-43, 74-75, 88, 92, 94, 112, 143, 147; differences with Harold Hughes over party structure, 113-16; elected to State Central Committee (1956), 59; and Jake More, 59-60; as Democratic Party Chairman, 71, 90-91; voter identification techniques, 42, 129.
Hazleton, 97, 99-100, 102, 104.
Hedberg, Art, 43, 147.
Herring, Clyde E., 50.
Herring, Clyde L., 12, 50, 59.
Hickenlooper, Bourke, 46, 88-89.
Hoegh, Leo, 48, 91; and farm vote, 57, 75; gubernatorial campaign of 1954, 48, 50; gubernatorial campaign of 1956, 54, 58, 74-75; legislative program, 51; and liquor laws, 57; and organized labor, 49-50; and sales tax, 56; "scorecards" for legislators, 51.
Hoffa, Jimmy, 62.
Hotel Fort Des Moines, 42, 61.
Hughes, Harold E., 2, 8, 68, 71, 73, 88, 92; and Amish education controversy of 1965-66, 96-105, 107-09; chooses not to run for re-election (1974), 77, 84; Christian principles, 83-84; and Iowa General Assembly, 85-94; gubernatorial campaign of 1962, 77, 87; gubernatorial campaign of 1966, 117; and Lex Hawkins, 74, 113-16; and la-

INDEX

bor, 110-13; and national party reform, 8, 121; political background, 77, 79-80, 144, 155; political style, 8, 78-79, 81-82, 118-21, 164, 171; and race relations, 96, 107, 120; and Park Rinard, 79-81; and social reform, 82-84, 86, 95, 119; U.S. Senate campaign of 1968, 122-24.
Hultman, Evan, 92.
Human Rights Commission, Iowa, 120.
Humphrey, Hubert, 123.
Hybrid seed corn, 23.

Ida Grove, 83.
Immigrants, 14.
Independents, 128, 143, 162, 165, 172-73.
Industry, Iowa, 7, 21, 58; productivity, 26; safety law, 119.
Inheritance tax, 95.
Initiative (political reform), 6.
Interest groups, 11-12, 16, 20-21, 29.
Iowa, Code of, 31, 82.
Iowa, Constitution of, 32.
Iowa, General Assembly of, 42, 70, 108, 123, 127; Fifty-eighth (1959), 109; Fifty-ninth (1961), 75; Sixtieth (1963), 85-87; Sixty-first (1965), 94-95, 112-13.
Iowa, House of Representatives of, 4, 46-48, 70.
Iowa, State Capitol of, 17, 32, 48, 51, 82.
Iowa, State Commerce Commission of, 80.
Iowa, State Senate of, 46, 48, 70.
Iowa, State Superintendent of Schools of, 108.
Iowa, State Supreme Court of, 171.
Iowa Bar Association, 20.
Iowa Farm Bureau Federation (IFBF): growth of, 16-18; "know your candidates" meetings, 19; and labor unions, 11-12, 31-33; and reapportionment, 65-67, 75-76, 86, 91; and Republican Party, 20-21, 46, 56-57; and taxes, 30; and USDA, 17-18.
Iowa Federation of Labor, 11, 49, 53.
Iowa Legislative Research Bureau, 64.
Iowa Manufacturers Association (IMA): and farmers, 57; and labor unions, 11-12, 32, 50-52, 109-10; and reapportionment, 34, 67-68; and Republican Party, 16-17, 21, 46, 48, 62, 75, 91; and taxes, 30, 56.
Iowa Medical Society, 20.
Iowa Republican Labor Council, 49-50.
Iowa State Education Association, 20, 107.
Iowa State University, 61, 87.
Iowa Temperance Legislative Council, 51.
Iowa Voters Committee, 168, 171.

Jackson County, 135, 163, 166.
Johnson, Lyndon, 92, 116, 118, 120, 155, 161-62.
Johnson, Robert M. L., 161-63.
Johnston, Robert L., 40, 43, 52.

INDEX

Jones County, 135.
Judd, Walter N., 161.

Kaufman, Andy, 104.
Kennedy, Edward M., 141-42, 149-50, 161; 1962 senatorial campaign, 118, 147.
Kennedy, Joan, 149.
Kennedy, John F., 69-70, 78, 89, 142.
Keokuk, 88.
Key clubs, 31, 38, 82. *See also* Liquor laws.
Kimball, Ed, 17.
King, Karl, 79.
King, Larry L., 119.
Kotz, Nick (*Des Moines Register*), 85.

Labor laws, 30-31, 49, 50-53, 61, 67, 70; opposition to, 31.
Labor unions, 7, 50-53; and Democratic Party coalition, 46, 49-53, 146; membership in Iowa, 11, 19; in state politics, 16, 19-20, 49-53, 131; support for reapportionment, 66.
La Follette, Robert M., 6.
Larrabee, William, 5-6.
Larson, Cliff, 131, 168.
League of Iowa Municipalities, 42, 81.
League of Women Voters, 42, 66-67.
Lemon, Harlan, 103.
Less, Frank, 142, 145, 148.
Linn County, 135-36, 138, 142, 163.
Liquor laws, 30-31, 48, 51, 57-58, 67, 70, 77-79, 86, 91.

Loveless, Herschel C., 53f, 80, 84; appointed to Federal Renegotiation Board (1960), 70; and farm vote, 57; gubernatorial campaign of 1956, 54, 56, 58; gubernatorial campaign of 1958, 61-63; and labor unions, 53-54; and liquor laws, 57-58; and Jake More, 159-60; and political appointments, 59-60; political background, 54-56; U.S. Senate campaign of 1960, 68-70; and vice-presidency (1960), 69.

Manufacturers in politics, *see* Iowa Manufacturers Association.
Manufacturing employment, 26.
Maquoketa *Jackson Sentinel,* 159.
Martin, Thomas E., 68.
McCarthy, Eugene, 120, 164.
McGovern, George, 121, 133-34, 171.
McManus, Edward M., 67-68.
McMartin, Cole, 166-67.
McNary-Haugen bills, 7.
Meat packing companies, 6.
Mezvinsky, Edward, 171.
Miller, Jack, 133, 165, 168, 171; 1960 campaign, 68-70; 1966 campaign, 116.
Miller, Norman, 49.
Mills, Ray, 49, 53.
Minimum wage laws, 53.
Minority groups, 96, 120.
Missouri, 26.
Mitchell, Donald J., 13, 57.
Mobile registrars, 173.
Monetary policies, inflationary, 4.

INDEX
— 213 —

Monopolies, 4. See also Anti-Monopoly Party.
More, Jake, 12-16, 59-62, 68; and Harry Truman, 15; opposed by Des Moines Democratic leaders (1954), 45; ousted from Democratic Party chairmanship (1958), 45, 59-61; and party leadership, 13-15, 40, 59-60, 70; and patronage, 12-16.
Murray, William G., 61, 68, 108.
Muscatine, 122, 127.
Muskie, Edmund, 173.

National Plowing Match, 15.
National Young Democrats, 45.
Neighborhood registration sites, 42, 130.
New Deal, 3, 7, 127, 137.
Nixon, Richard M., 161, 164, 167; and presidential campaigns, 69, 122-23, 133; and Watergate, 128, 175.
Non-Partisan Citizens Committee for a Constitutional Convention, 67.
Norberg, Duke, 60-62, 70.
Nye, Frank (*Cedar Rapids Gazette*), 59, 86.

O'Brien, Lawrence, 159, 162.
Oelwein *Daily Register,* 158.
Old Order Amish, *see* Amish education controversy of 1965.
Oleomargarine debate (1952), 48.
Open housing law, 120.
Open shop, *see* Labor laws.
Ottumwa, 27, 54.
Owens, Edris, 52-53, 60, 90.

Page County, 39.
Parks and public recreation, 119.
Parties, political, 33, 47, 50, 128. See also Democratic Party, Republican Party, Third party movements.
Party leaning, 129.
Patronage, political, 12-14, 38-39; federal appointments, 12-13, 40; Grand Jury appointments in Polk County, 38; role of county chairmen in, 14.
Patrons of Husbandry, 4.
Payne, Sereno E., 6.
Penal reforms, 95.
Perkins, Charles Eliot, 4.
Peterson, H. Rand, 91.
Pierson, Donald C., 52.
Plambeck, Herb, 15.
Political machines, 13-14.
Polk County, 27, 37.
Polk County Board of Supervisors, 37, 45.
Polk County Democrats, 2, 147-48; in the 1950s, 42-46, 63, 71, 135; in the 1960s, 74, 90, 117-18.
Polk County Farm, 39.
Polk County Grand Jury, 38.
Population trends in Iowa, 21, 23, 26.
Populists, 3, 5, 8.
Postville, 153.
Poverty program, 165.
Precinct caucuses, 19, 128.
Primary election, 6, 19.
Progressives, 6-7, 34.
Progressive Republicans, 3-5.
Protective Association (Farmers'), 4.

INDEX

Public ownership of railroads and utilities, 7.

Race relations, 73.
Railroads: railroad barons, 3, 16; in politics, 5-6; regulation by Iowa legislature, 4; taxes on, 6.
Rasmussen, Clark, 115, 131.
Ray, Robert D., 91, 127, 151, 175; 1968 gubernatorial campaign, 123; 1970 gubernatorial campaign, 125; political style, 124-25.
Reagan, Ronald, 173.
Reapportionment, in Iowa: 1904 state constitutional amendments, 64; 1928 state constitutional amendments, 64; federal plan, 64; history in Iowa, 33-34, 41, 91; legislative debate of 1955, 63-66; legislative debate of 1958, 63-66; and partisanship, 58-59, 63, 65-68, 75, 87, 109; temporary and permanent plans of 1963, 85-87, 144; and urban-rural conflict, 30-32, 64-67. See also Shaff Plan.
Recall, 6.
Referendum, 6.
Registration cities, 42.
Reno, Milo, 7.
Republican Party, and Democratic voter registration efforts, 131; economic philosophy, 16; and interest groups, 16, 29; intraparty rifts, 75; and labor unions, 16, 49-51, 113; membership, 122; organizational strength, 16; Polk County organization, 37; progressive elements in, 3, 46-51, 91; state conventions, 47, 49-51; state platforms, 47-50.
Reuther, Walter, 40.
Right-to-work laws, 31-32, 47, 49-50, 53, 56, 96, 109, 112, 122; and Iowa Manufacturers Association, 109.
Riley, Tom, 163-64, 167.
Rinard, Park, 80-81, 110, 112.
Road use taxes, 30.
Roosevelt, Franklin D., 7, 143.
Roosevelt Hotel (Cedar Rapids), 147.
Rotten boroughs, 33.

Sales tax, 30, 54, 58-59, 62-63.
Savery Hotel (Des Moines), 42.
Scalise, Lawrence, 103.
School financing, 33.
School redistricting, 33.
Schwengel, Fred, 171.
Scranton, William, 91.
Second Congressional District of Iowa, 135-37.
Senatorial elections, see Elections.
Sensor, Arthur, 97.
Service clubs, 31.
Shaff, David O., 66.
Shaff Plan (for legislative reapportionment), 66, 75, 82, 86, 109, 144. See also Reapportionment.
Shelby County, 12.
Shriver, R. Sargent, 149.
Smith, E. B., 1962 U.S. Senate campaign, 87-89; 1966 U.S. Senate campaign, 116.
Smith, Neal, 59-60, 87, 92, 115,

INDEX
— 215 —

123; 1966 Congressional campaign, 40, 45.
Smith-Lever Act, 17.
Split-ticket voting, 128.
Standpatter Republicans, 3, 5, 6.
Stanley, David, 127, 172; criticizes campaign opponent Harold Hughes (1968), 122.
State aid to schools, 95.
State education laws, and community compliance, 99-100, 102.
State income tax, 30.
State income tax check-off law, 132.
Stevenson, Adlai E., 57.
Stock market, 6.
Suburbanization, 25.
Suckow, Ruth, 28-29.
Sullivan, Leo, 159.

Taft, William H., 6.
Taft-Hartley Act, 31, 113.
Talle, Henry O., 136-38, 160.
Tariff reform, 6, 54, 58-59.
Taxes, 30, 56, 61-63, 67, 75, 95, 119.
Teamsters Union, 62-63.
Television, use in political camppaign, 89.
Thatcher, Kenneth, 18.
Third party movements, 3; tradition in Iowa, 34.
Truman, Harry S., 7, 12, 15, 46.

Unemployment compensation laws, 49.
Union Army, 3.
Union shops, 31, 47, 49, 58, 110, 112. *See also* Labor unions.

United Auto Workers, 20, 40, 43, 89; financial assistance for voter registration, 90.
U.S. Census Bureau, 12, 25.
U.S. Department of Agriculture, 12, 17.
U.S. Post Office, 12.
U.S. Senate Foreign Affairs Committee, 89.
U.S. Supreme Court, 95.
Upper Iowa University, 143.
Urbanization in Iowa, 21; and employment, 26-28; political consequences, 28-29, 31, 85; and voting patterns, 7, 8, 23, 25, 28-29.

Verba, Sidney, 79.
Vietnam, 8, 73, 108, 116, 120, 123, 161, 164-65.
Voter Identification Program, 129, 165, 168, 172. *See also* Democratic Party.
Voter registration, 130-31.
Voting requirements, 130-31.

Walking decks, 166, 173.
Wall, Joseph Frazier, 7.
Wallace, George, 123.
Wapello, 27.
Washington, Iowa, 6.
Watergate, 128, 131, 134, 171, 175.
Waterloo, 65, 120.
Waukon, 146.
Weaver, General James B., 4-5.
Weimer, J. D., 144.
Wells, Kenneth, 107.
West Union *Argo-Gazette,* 150.
Whitney, Tom, 172.

INDEX

Winneshiek, 135.
WMT-TV (Cedar Rapids), 166.
Wolf, Leonard G., 137, 141, 148, 160.
Wood, Grant, 80.
Workmen's compensation laws, 54.
World War II, 85, 94, 120, 128; and political careers, 48, 80, 83; and the rise of interest groups, 11, 18, 20.

A lifelong resident of Iowa City, JAMES C. LAREW *began research for* A Party Reborn *as a history student preparing for his honors thesis at Harvard College. Upon graduation, Larew furthered his study of Iowa history and politics while serving as political assistant to Iowa Senator John C. Culver in Washington and in Iowa. Larew now works for the Larew Company, a family-owned plumbing and heating business, and resides with his wife Mary and his grandfather Telford Larew in Iowa City.*